Justice Under God

ISBN 978-1-958659-16-8

Christopher J. Muse

JUSTICE UNDER GOD

How Faith, Hope, and Charity
Freed an Innocent Man and
Helped Save a Thousand Lives

Combray House

He hath showed thee, O man, what is good; and what doth the LORD require of thee, but to do justly, and to love mercy, and to walk humbly with thy God?

Micah 6:8

Every subject of the commonwealth ought to find a certain remedy, by having recourse to the laws, for all injuries or wrongs, which he may receive in his person, property, or character. He ought to obtain right and justice freely, and without being obliged to purchase it; completely, and without any denial; promptly, and without delay; conformably to the laws.

John Adams
Massachusetts Declaration of Rights, ARTICLE 1I

I know there is not enough justice out there, so I try to bring justice to the streets.

Bobby Joe Leaster

Introduction

JUG is an acronym for *Justice Under God* and is the code of conduct for Jesuit High Schools throughout the United States. It provides punishment for every transgression short of shooting a priest, and was usually imposed for tardiness, missed homework, skipping class, profanity, boisterousness, and that all-inclusive bad attitude. It began with a *"Muse, You're Jugged"* and ended with after school detention writing drivel a hundred times, cleaning the classrooms, or sprucing up the campus. I wrote *Lord Chesterfield's Definition of a Gentleman* on the blackboard so many times that I still have chalk under my fingernails. While that experience with JUG spawned the title *Justice Under God,* this book is not about adolescents coming of age.

I was 28 years old and a freshly minted lawyer when I got involved with my father, Robert F. Muse, in trying to overturn the wrongful conviction for murder and armed robbery and the life-time imprisonment of Bobby Joe Leaster. I had the confidence of youth and the optimism born of my absolute faith in the Massachusetts criminal justice system, so that, equipped with the toolbox of the law, and with study, effort, and persuasion, I *knew* that within time Bobby Joe would be freed.

I was a lawyer for 25 years before I was appointed a Justice of the Massachusetts Superior Court. I had a diverse practice that got me into nearly all the courts in Massachusetts almost every day, for over forty years. Courthouses are filled with life, drama, pathos, humor, failure, and success. I loved going into every one of them for the comradery and, when finished doing the serious business, the entertainment found in them. The *court*, not the building, is the engine of justice, and I saw every moving part of that goliath of a machine– in other words the thousands of staff, police, lawyers and judges. There is no louder cheerleader of it and them than me. They, collectively, do the heavy lifting of society's task of promoting fairness and integrity as they collectively pursue equal justice under law. But it is a human enterprise. It is not perfect. Mistakes are too often made.

In a perfect world, Justice, as we have learned from philosophers and patriots, would be a straight highway with parallel lanes for the Law, Morality, Ethics, and maybe with Conscience in the breakdown lane. But it is not a perfect world, and while the Law intersects those other lanes, it does not always converge and is in fact often on a collision course. Simply recall that our Constitution permitted enslavement and disenfranchised women until changed by the abolitionists and the suffragettes. We hold present memories of Civil Rights activists in confrontation with the law, risking and suffering violence, including death, The ultimate example of the stress point between morality and the law can be found in death penalty appeals where one's conscience is truly on a collision course with the Constitution.

Before this introduction I quoted the prophet Micah and the Due Process clause of the Massachusetts State Constitution. Those quotes were reminders of what judges were under oath to do and were pasted on the desk area of the bench in courtroom 1006 in Suffolk Superior Court which I shared with another Justice. My partner is a woman of profound faith. She selected the Micah quote. I am more secular and wordier and found John Adams' Article 11 a better fit for me.

It took nearly ten years of filing motions and pressing appeals in our state and federal courts before Bobby Joe Leaster escaped his hideously wrongful imprisonment. But it was not done because of the courts. His trial attorney, the prosecutor, and the police investigators were disappointments. The appellate courts neglected him. How he finally earned his freedom is what most of this book is about. As he often asked, "How did I get a fair trial if I am innocent?"

Bobby Joe believed, and expressed hundreds of times in public forums, that it was the hand of God, *The Good Master Above Us,* that delivered him to freedom. I always saw luck, serendipity, and pretty good lawyering as the causes, but I have almost changed my mind: *"Maybe, it was God."*

Faith in God sustained Bobby Joe during those cruel years. But he also believed that God sent him his lawyers and that as one bit of new evidence after another was obtained and other breaks in the case happened, it was because God was looking over his soul.

For thirty years Bobby worked with the most at-risk young men in the most troubled neighborhoods in Boston. As a youth worker, with the street cred of more than 15 years in prison and the most generous heart of any human being I have ever met, Bobby mentored and guided hundreds of kids who clung to gangs and travelled in the wrong direction. He attended hundreds of youth funerals, sometimes to provide security, but usually to grieve for someone he tried to help.

In 1993, Bobby Joe was part of the core team of street workers that brought the leaders of neighborhood gangs to the table to negotiate a truce that created an unprecedented ceasefire and for 27 months, a reduction of youth homicides to zero. It became a national model, famously described as the *Boston Miracle*. A few street workers addressed the most urgent requirement for social justice– public safety, and did so, with the ultimate reference to divinity, *miraculously*. As he went about mentoring young and disadvantaged men– some outcasts because they wore gang colors, others just "lost"– counseling them, finding them jobs, pushing them to remain in school, to keep out of prison, to stay alive, Bobby Joe Leaster, as much as any judge, lawyer, cleric, or social worker, served the mission defined by the rule of law and its elusive goal, *Justice*.

This was his mantra: *I know there is not enough justice out there, so I try to bring justice to the streets.*

How Bobby Joe received his own justice and promoted it a hundredfold, how my father more than anyone else fought for it, and how that experience shaped this young lawyer who became an older and hopefully wiser judge, is the rest of the story.

December 3, 2012, Boston, MA

As the police officer halted all traffic, the hearse turned from Commonwealth Avenue into the reserved space in front of St. Ignatius Church. The seats inside were filled by hundreds of friends and relatives of the deceased, gathered to respect the memory of a husband, father, grandfather, friend, extraordinary lawyer and, as was often repeated, a great guy.

An honor guard of six crisply uniformed Marines stood in formation to allow the hearse to stop so they could open it and with reverence remove the casket.

At that moment, the Marines were honoring Lieutenant Robert F. Muse, a member of Squadron 323, the storied *Death Rattlers* of World War II, who in May 1944 flew into a fusillade of bullets from the turret of a navy destroyer, aimed at the fast-approaching Japanese kamikaze pilot, who was within seconds of bringing certain destruction to the ship and death and injury to its sailors. Lieutenant Muse took out the enemy aircraft, aborting the suicide mission and escaping any harm from the so-called friendly fire of the United States Navy. His oldest daughter Mary would later that morning eulogize the dad who saved many lives aboard a ship and another.

His fellow Marines walked the casket up the steps of the church in perfect cadence and gently placed it on a resting spot at the back to be blessed. As the organist began her music, the pallbearers escorted the casket up the center aisle. Seven sons and two sons-in-law marched on either side. Pushing the casket was an African American man who could not hold back his tears or mute his sobs. This pallbearer, Bobby Joe Leaster, called Mr. Muse his dad, and all the other pallbearers his brothers.

Just two weeks earlier Bobby Joe visited with Bob Muse at his nearby Chestnut Hill home, taking time from his work with Boston's at-risk youth, to spend precious moments with a man he says saved his life. Bob Muse explained the pride he had for his surrogate son:

"You left the bitterness behind and made something of yourself. You gave back to a city that took so much from you."

Bobby Joe Leaster took his frail hand and told him, "Thanks, Dad. Everything I did, I did to honor you."

September 27, 1970, Dorchester, MA

The rain fell off and on since mid-morning, and even though it was just a drizzle it made for a gray September Sunday afternoon in the mostly black Codman Square section of Dorchester, Massachusetts. Thirteen-year-old Mark Johnson was determined to get out of his house on Colonial Ave. and just do something with his friends.

Eddie Simmons was coming down from Millet Street and joined Mark as they decided to do "something" together, the something that thirteen-year-old kids needed to do to fight off the boredom of a rainy Sunday afternoon. They were walking through an empty lot behind their friend Stewey Loughtman's house. They then walked down Mallard Street to go to the Talbot Variety store, when Mrs. Whiteside came running out, screaming, "Levi is dead!"

After a while, Simmons and Mark walked back toward the same place they had come from. A policeman happened to be nearby when Mark said, "They ran into the house."

"What did you say?" the cop asked.

"I said nothin'," Mark would later insist he replied.

Chapter One

CHRIS MUSE

In March 1977, I left my law office in Downtown Crossing, Boston, and drove to Norfolk Prison. I was going there to meet Bobby Joe Leaster who was serving time for a murder and armed robbery that occurred on September 27, 1970. All I knew about his case, which was very little, came from reading the Supreme Judicial Court decision that found that his conviction and life sentence without the possibility of parole was lawful. I was travelling to meet him to prepare an appeal to the Federal Court.

I was familiar with the road to Norfolk. It passed the town I grew up in, Brookline Massachusetts, not the leafy Chestnut Hill section, but the pre-gentrified Coolidge Corner area which was a bit more diverse and edgy. The Coolidge Corner Theater showed Saturday cartoons and Batman movies for a quarter. Now it is the regionally famous independent cultural film venue. The First National supermarket is a bookstore. Pelham Drug is a Mexican restaurant. Brigham's Ice Cream shop is long gone.

One of eleven children of two smart and accomplished parents, I grew up in what is best described as managed chaos. It was the organized chaos you see on the floor of the New York Stock Exchange, after the trading bell rings. We were all loved, properly clothed and fed, and generally well-supervised, but the decibel level and the constant bickering ending often in pushing, shoving, and punching, can best be described as chaotic. Fueled by attention neediness and in some measure testosterone, there was unrelenting teasing and annoying behavior among toddlers, prepubescents, and pimply teenagers. Anyone who thinks "Brady Bunch" for this size family, is over -medicated. But, for all of the chaos, there was no better place to grow up.

There was of course some order in the Muse household; dinners every night at six; spaghetti on Wednesday; fish on Friday; hot dogs and beans on Saturday; and roast beef on Sundays. Lunches were peanut butter and jelly or baloney sandwiches in brown bags.

The real source of order for those eleven lives was St. Aidan's, the parish, and the school, run by the Sisters of St. Joseph, best known as the original parish of John F. Kennedy. He would be "the first Catholic president of the United States" we were told, as the nuns guided us through prayers during the fall of 1960. I like to think that my *Our Fathers* put him over the top in November and was disappointed to learn it was Mayor Daley and his Chicago political machine.

Most of my friends lived close to the school or nearby in the Egmont Street projects. These were the rows of apartments built for the returning veterans of World War Two. It housed those members of the Greatest Generation who became firemen, cops, office workers and laborers. It was a pretty good and safe place to play and hang out after school. My friend Jimmy Esposito's father was a car salesman, and Billy Connolly's dad was a fireman.

Like most grammar schools, St. Aidan's was painfully boring. God had a prominent place, and his message and directives were often repeated. The Baltimore Catechism was a sourcebook for clean moral living. We learned every variety of sin contemplated by the Ten Commandments, with impure thoughts and touching getting considerable play. We spent a lot of time memorizing states and capitals in our geography books, singing from Gregorian Chant books, reading comprehension exercises and history chapters I have forgotten. I excelled at declining sentences and solving arithmetic problems. I needed improvement with penmanship and conduct.

The parochial schools were feeders for Catholic high schools. Eighth grade was prep time for the exams. I passed the one for the elite Boston College High School and joined my brothers Michael and Robert there the following fall. At BC High I joined the ranks of more than three hundred students in what can best be described as a boot camp adventure, becoming great friends with many who were wonderful young men. Most everyone had problems with the four-year Latin requirement. It is a dead language, where the verb is placed at the end of the sentence, and adjectives and adverbs are placed nowhere close to the nouns and verbs they modified. This was an impossible subject for a kid who was a super star at declining sentences. The Jesuits were strict disciplinarians. While my penmanship improved, my conduct did not.

Lady Luck guided my application to Georgetown University. This was before Patrick Ewing brought the Hoyas to the Final Four and a national championship, causing applications to soar at the new "IT" school. I had an incredible four years, although not shown in my grades, which admittedly, were average, arguably mediocre. But the education and the experience, to borrow a French expression, a language dearer to me than Latin, was *nonpareil.*

I had 16 years of Catholic education, eight with the Sisters of St. Joseph, and another eight with the Jesuits. My general takeaway is that the priests explained the gospel, but the nuns lived it. For all my years of mandatory religious instruction, only the Ten Commandments and Jesus's sermon on the Mount remain as my religious guideposts, with some influence from the Jesuits' dictum to be "a man for others."

The nuns at St. Aidan's often cautioned us that everything we said or did was recorded in heaven. This was way before gigabytes and the digital age. We imagined many monks with flowing beards recording every impure thought and other major transgressions in huge scrolls, high above the celestial clouds, in our individual *Permanent Records.* Notwithstanding any entries indicating laziness or inattentiveness or any indicia of mediocrity, I was accepted at the best evening division law school in the country. Something set me on fire at Suffolk Law, as I was enjoying my classes, getting superior grades, loving the study of law, and being proud as a peacock when I was sworn in as a lawyer.

This brings me to that date and time when my life and Bobby Joe Leaster's life changed in many different ways.

1969, REFORM, PICKENS COUNTY, ALABAMA

Thirty miles from Tuscaloosa, State Highway 82 going west towards Mississippi intersects with Route 17 and forms the four corners of the center of Reform Alabama. Its population, according to the 1970 US census was 1893 adults and children, half Black and half White. The surrounding Pickens County had just over 20,000 inhabitants. Legend has it that Reform received its name from a travelling evangelist who promised not to return until its people reformed. The dusty roads and limited downtown invited the predictable description—*a sleepy southern town.* Bobby Joe's boyhood friend Jimmy Johnson said Reform "was slow moving. Plenty of time to think. Nothing to rush to." Like all towns and counties in the deep south, Reform and Pickens had a history of enslavement, the rule of Jim Crow, and a culture of segregation.

On the way to Reform, you passed acres of cotton and corn fields worked by sharecroppers who survived by the back-breaking field work of the parents and their children who had little beyond crowded housing in the ramshackle cabins that dotted the rural landscape. Every day, in the words of that dated song, they got "a little bit older and deeper in debt." The credit system was the bedrock of the farm economy. Sharecroppers rented their plots on credit and obtained their seeds and supplies the same way. Once their crops were harvested and sold, the landowners called in the rents they were due and the equipment and farm stores were paid, and little remained for necessities, much less, niceties.

Johnny Benton, one of 16 children raised 5 miles from Hopewell High, who went to school only when he was not harvesting cotton or corn, recalled, "There was plenty of food and we never meant to want for nothing." He and Floyd Hurst, who also grew up on a farm, were classmates of Bobby Joe. Floyd was a strong athlete who enrolled in school the day after Labor Day, then stayed away to harvest- first the cotton, then the corn and also the peanuts and onions, until mid-November. Still, even though he was absent from school all week, he was eligible to play football on Friday nights.

Bobby Joe and his nephews that he called brothers, Earl, and Andrew, though not raised on a farm, still *enjoyed* the pleasures of the fall harvest. Until Bobby Joe's mother got a job cleaning the Hopewell School, he, Andrew, and Earl would rise early to wait on the side of the road to jump on a flatbed truck that delivered them to fields to pick cotton until 5:00 PM. They were paid 8 to 10 cents for a hundred pounds of cotton, earning 10 to 15 cents a day. In a week they saved enough to go to Tuscaloosa on Saturdays to buy tennis shoes and clothes. Andrew chuckled as he recalled the teachers taking attendance, those autumn days;

"Bobby Joe Leaster ?"	"Picking cotton!"
"Earl Leaster ?"	"Picking cotton!"
"Andrew Leaster?"	"Picking cotton!"

~

The trees from the woods around Reform were logged and trucked to nearby sawmills that ended up in lumber yards and hardware stores close by. Bobby Joe's father drove a truck for one of the hardware stores and delivered lumber and sometimes seed to local customers.

18

The lucky man who escaped the heavy labor of farming or logging usually ended up at the Dr. Pepper plant, driving a truck to stores and schools to load up the soft drink machines, like Jimmy Johnson, or doing maintenance work at the town buildings and hospitals, like Johnny Benton. There were few other opportunities. Bobby's basketball teammate, Larry Richardson, listed three: "You went into the army; you went up north to the plants and factories; you went to college; and that was mostly for some girls."

Until Bobby Joe was in tenth grade, William Hayes and Leana Leaster rented a wood framed two room and kitchen house from a White man as no Blacks owned homes. It was on the other side of Route 82 near a sawmill. There was no indoor plumbing, but an outhouse in the backyard, next to a large wood-fired kettle used both for bathing and for the washing clothes that were dried on a line. Kerosene lamps gave off light in the shack's interior that was not wired for electricity. There were no street names. The house was on a dirt road and visitors were given directions such as, "Come up the hill and turn when you see…." Everyone called Bobby "Joe." His mother was affectionately called "Puney" and his father was simply "Hayes."

Hayes and Puney took the bedroom and Bobby Joe and his nephews Willie Earl and Andrew camped out in the other room on a couch, a bed, and blankets on the floor. The nephews were the sons of his sister Fanny Lou who moved to Detroit when Andrew was two years old and Earl was four. "Puney took us from our real momma because my step daddy was always jumping on my mother" Andrew recalled. Puney treated all three the same, so Bobby always referred to them as his brothers.

The all-black Hopewell School, a five-minute walk from his home, was the center of Joe's world. When the family moved to a nearby housing project of single level duplex homes built for thirty families, the Leasters had indoor plumbing and clean running water. Bobby Joe had a larger group of friends nearby, and a few steps from his doorway, a basketball court. It was just a basket, or anything that looked like a basket, that the boys nailed to a post on the street. If Bobby was not in school or in his house, he was pumping balls into that basket.

Jimmy Johnson lived next door to the Leasters, and Larry Richardson just a few houses away. They and the Leaster brothers were constantly on the court. Larry was closer in age to Andrew, who Larry remembers was a three-sport star athlete. Except for Earl, they all played together at Hopewell High School, all were good, but Bobby was the star. He led the team in scoring as a junior and a senior and brought it to regional tournaments. "He had a great fade away jump shot," Floyd Hurst recalled, "White people came to watch him. He was that good."

When they first played an all-White team from either Hubbertville or Fayette, Team Captain Johnny Benton was lectured by the referee at the start of the game and told to follow his commands: "Now go back and tell your Black buddies what I told you." Predictably, the ref quickly and unfairly fouled out Bobby Joe and their star center. As Hopewell went down in defeat, Bobby accepted it without rancor or comment. Johnny Benton said "Joe was just a wonderful person, a great athlete, quiet and humble. He was a good person, never got angry."

When shown a picture of him in a fifth-grade classroom, in the 1963 Hopewell Owls yearbook, Bobby Joe said, "Yes, I was smiling, and I felt good at that time," but things were very difficult.

"We were dirt poor, not a lot of money. My mother was a domestic, cleaning White peoples' houses. My dad worked in a hardware store. My mother worked all day, and she was still at work when we came home from school. She always returned at 6:00 with a whole lot of packages and stuff and extra food. She worked for Miss Martha, a White lady with 2 or 3 kids. She was not rich, just regular. Me and my nephews would go there after school and play out back Sometimes we went to a convenience store around the corner from my house. It was owned by a white guy. My mother had a credit there and we could get candy and stuff after school."

"Puney" in the words of Andrew, was "good and kind. She took in neighbors and would cook for anyone: She could be heard saying, 'Come in here and lay on the couch,' or 'You need something to eat?" She took her boys to church on Sundays and delivered them to bible classes after services. She made sure they helped the church by cleaning the cemetery or doing other tasks.

His friends called Bobby Joe a "momma's boy." It meant that he obeyed everything she demanded. He was not a sissy; in fact, he was known to be tough. So, while there was plenty of mischief, Bobby engaged in little. Andrew and the boys often broke into Hopewell's gym to play basketball, sometimes taking chocolate milk and cheeses out of the cafeteria. Larry Richardson sometimes tried to steal Hayes' bootleg liquor. "He'd yell at us, 'stay away from my homebrew' or shout, 'Who stole my home-brew'? "But Joe did not drink. Nor did he smoke the rabbit tobacco which had no nicotine and was made from the leaves of a sweet local plant. Being a 'momma's boy" described respect, not weakness.

My mother was very religious, and she made sure we went to Church every Sunday. We had one hour of Sunday School, and the church all day until 3:00 or 4:00. My mother and father taught me to believe in God and have faith. It was instilled in me. I can still hear my mother to this day saying, 'God is the Supreme Being and always have faith in God.' Today I feel the same way.

When she got the job cleaning Hopewell School, Puney made sure her three boys attended daily. She easily enforced that rule with Bobby and Andrew, who could not play sports if they did not attend school. Earl was a challenge: he was not active with sports, had little game time on the project's basketball court, and no interest in anything except making money, however little that might be. He had difficulty in school because "the Black schools were not like today. If in the first grade you were not ready for the second grade, you were sent to it any way. I was not learning what I should. I was still at a fourth-grade level in the ninth grade. I stopped going to school. I played hooky."

Puney stepped in. "I heard about Job Corps. I asked Puney to sign me up. That would get me out of Reform. I had to leave to make a better life." Puney gave Earl money to travel to Missoula Montana where he spent two years at a job training facility, learning to cook, and earning a G.E.D. Afterward, it was off to Boston to join cousins Gladys, Inez, and Ruby.

Dad was the opposite of Puney. "Monday to Thursday he was a good person," Earl observed.

"He worked every single day. He gave his money to my grandmother. Nights he listened to the radio, sometimes watched TV, and read the paper. And though he avoided church on Sundays, he was a man of faith, like almost all the Black men in Reform. On Friday he would take a shower and then go out for the weekend. He would drink his homebrew and gamble at cards and dice. We did not talk to him much, but we respected him."

~

Everyone in town knew Hayes Leaster. Johnny Benton was scared of the man he described as 'tough.' Larry Richardson recalled him as 'stern': "It was "because of slavery. You know, kids over here, adults over there, mentality," that explained his disengagement. Hayes did not watch Bobby Joe or Andrew play basketball, even in the tournaments, though their sisters would travel from Florida to cheer them on. Andrew called his grandfather a "hellcat on Fridays" to explain his absence on those game nights.

Hopewell School had every grade in its one building: Grades 1 to 6 were on one side; Grades 7 to 12 were located on the other. There was a gymnasium, a cafeteria, a study hall, and a sparse library, with encyclopedias and few books, overseen by the dedicated Ms. Beenion. "She read a lot and talked about opportunities," Larry Richardson fondly recalled.

Bobby learned to read with limitation and to write very poorly. There was no emphasis on studying as there was little expectation that Hopewell's students would go beyond high school. The exception was for some of the girls. There were Black women teachers with college degrees who encouraged promising young women to study and enroll in the Black colleges scattered throughout the South. But the boys? They just needed to pass the courses. Since Bobby Joe was a basketball star, little more than "D" grades were required.

Bobby Joe thrived on the basketball court. Coach Oliver put him on the varsity team as a freshman, and as a senior he was the top scoring player during a winning season, losing few times, and somehow getting the attention of the coach of the all- Black Jackson State College across the state line in eastern Mississippi.

Coach Oliver, white and young, was a recent graduate of Alabama State which he attended on a baseball scholarship. Besides army recruiters, he was one of the few white men who came to Hopewell. He coached basketball by default but produced top caliber teams. He took care of his players. He bought them basketball shoes with his personal money. Andrew remembers the Converse high tops that he wore only for games which he shelved afterwards, replaced by the tennis shoes for everyday use. And he guided Bobby Joe Leaster to basketball excellence.

There were never any newspaper articles about our teams, only for the White school teams. The coaches must have come to watch us and saw me, because there was always one scholarship to Jackson for a student from Hopewell, and I got it.

The all-White Pickens County High School was located a few miles and a clearly demarked world away from the Blacks on the Hopewell School side of Route 82. Not only could they not attend, the Blacks were kept away from the area surrounding the school.

Larry Richardson tolerated the segregation and the insulting racist names hurled at him. "Growing up it was ok. There was a sense of belonging. Everyone was in the same boat. But it stuck in my craw when young white people called Black adults by their first name. There was no respect. It pissed me off."

"Did it bother Bobby Joe to go to an all-Black school?"

I didn't care. That's all I knew.

But the rest of segregation, yes that bothered me. All the property was owned by Whites. All the businesses wore owned by Whites. There were "Whites only" signs everywhere. The laundromat was for just Whites. My mother had a kettle in the back yard to wash clothes. When you went to the Dairy Queen, you had to eat outside. When it rained just the White people could sit inside.

And they always called us Boy. Like "Whose Boy are you?."

If you were walking down the street and a White lady was walking towards you, we could not look at her, we had to drop our heads down. If you looked up, it was against the rules.

The White kids my age were racists. They were taught to hate Blacks. They were never friends with us. Nothing would happen between us, no fights or anything They just walked by us.

It was unfair to treat us that way. We were all human beings. They believe in God. We believe in God. .

They had "Whites Only" water fountains.

Did I ever drink from them?

ALL THE TIME!

Equal justice under law was elusive and mostly non-existent for Blacks. Jimmy Johnson remembers being accused of flirting with a white girl and getting locked up. "Someone wrote a letter and signed our names to it. The letter was written by a girl's father. It said we were going out with his daughter. It was false."

Johnny Benton's uncle went to prison because a white woman accused him of looking at her. "We had to stay in our place. Sometimes Blacks would get arrested and your White boss would pay to get you out of jail so you could go back to work. But he would hold back your money and say, 'I'll give half back (of wages) so you won't get in trouble again'."

Floyd Hurst remembers white people saying, "We are the law." This was never truer than when Bobby Joe's older brother William Hayes Jr., who everyone called *June Bug*, was killed. Bobby Joe painfully recalled that day:

He went to the corner store to buy cigarettes and put it on my mother's bill. He got into some altercation with the store owner and was shot in the chest, He stumbled out the front door around the corner. We were notified. I was 11, maybe 12 years old. We ran down to the corner. I saw my brother Jimmy holding June Bug in his arms and crying. June Bug was dead. There was only one policeman in Reform. He cleared the white man of the shooting. From that point on, all the Blacks in town boycotted that store.

We got through June Bug's killing like everything else, with prayer and with faith."

~

Bobby's friends and brothers remember the killing of Bobby Joe's big brother through a different lens, sometimes distorted because of time, and the absence of any written records available. As Jimmy Johnson recalls: "June Bug worked as a logger, cutting and trimming trees and putting them on trucks to make lumber. When he was not working, he drank a lot, and he could have been drinking when he went to Mr. Stevenson's store, took a pack of cigarettes and said to the owner's son, "put that on credit."

All the families had credit there. June Bug stuttered, so maybe he was not understood by the man who was white and prejudiced. Larry Richardson believes he was shot in the back with a .32. Others thought it was a shotgun. In any event, no one was charged by the white police officer. There was no investigation.

There were several days of protests at the store, and some talk of burning it. The boycott caused Stevenson to close the store and move away.

As Earl sadly stated, "He was killed for a pack of cigarettes. That's the way it was."

The Civil Rights movement- the protests and the marches- did little to change Bobby Joe's life in Reform through 1969. The Leasters owned a small black and white television but paid little attention to the national news of racial conflict, because as Bobby said, *"We were living it."* He does remember when he was younger watching Martin Luther King Jr. march down the main street in Reform. And Later, *I was in school when they said, they just shot Martin Luther King, and we all cried.*

Before Dr. King was assassinated, he and others in the movement were planning a Poor Peoples Campaign March to Washington to draw attention to the obvious. The plans included a Mule Train from Marks, Mississippi to Atlanta, and then to Washington by train. In spite of, or more likely fueled by Dr. King's death, the March began. Two months afterwards, mules pulled 15 wagons and 115 people through eastern Mississippi, into Central Alabama. In late May they stopped for two days in Reform. Bobby Joe's best memory of that historic journey was his mother bringing food, lots of food, to the marchers.

One year later Bobby Joe rejected the Jackson State scholarship and with his friend Jimmy Johnson boarded a greyhound bus in Reform to Tuscaloosa then Birmingham, then points north. He joined the migration that seemed to be preordained. By the time he reached high school, Bobby Joe's older brother and sisters had moved out.

Fanny Lou went to Detroit. Nancy. Daisey Mae, Katie Mae, Jimmy Lee left for Atlanta, Orlando, Chicago. I was sad leaving but felt excited to go to a big city to start a new life. I looked forward to it."

Puney handed him a large bag with sausage and bread, as she hugged her *Momma's Boy* goodbye, not knowing she would not hold him again for more than a dozen years.

MARCH 7, 1977

I remember driving my 1974 battleship gray Audi Fox to my father's law office when he gave me Bobby Joe's case.

It was Monday afternoon and I had just finished my first day of my first full week as a Middlesex County Indigent Defender.

The previous Tuesday I introduced myself to the judges and folks at the Third District Court of Eastern Middlesex as their new public defender. Judge Louie Glazer, a little guy, who off the bench, was always with a cigar in his hand or mouth, or within arm's reach, instructed me in the niceties of law practice not once heard in law school.

"I'm the Chief Justice in Malden, and I like to think that it's my responsibility to make sure things run smoothly." he said to me in his oversized office behind the first session court room. "I start at nine o' clock on the dot, and I expect everyone to be here and ready to work. I particularly do not like lawyers who are late."

Lesson one: Do not be tardy.

"Also, I consider myself a fair man, so that when you're putting your case in, remember this, and that I am not an idiot, and that you don't have to waste a lot of my time on foolishness."

Lesson two: No foolishness.

He indicated that it was time to leave. I made my way through the offices on the first floor. One by one, I met the magistrates, clerks, probation officers and bailiffs, prosecutors, and cops, and all the rest who made this train run on time.

By the end of my first day, I had learned that the jurisdiction of the court consisted of the half- dozen small blue collar and middle-class cities and towns that bordered the city of Malden. I would be handling the bulk of the misdemeanor cases of people who could not afford a lawyer. Drunk driving, trespass, wife beating (the term domestic violence was a few years away from currency), possession of drugs, usually marijuana, shop lifting, bad checks, daytime B&E's (breaking and enterings), and juvenile delinquency were on the index of offenses that I would defend.

During the next several days I took a seat behind the defense lawyer table and observed the administration of justice in the Malden District Court. Soon I would be handling arraignments. My criminal procedure books described this as the first critical stage of representation. This was when the lawyer filed his appearance and entered a plea of not guilty. He would argue for the release or reasonable bail of his client and would establish a schedule for the trial of the case. From the emphasis on the formality of arraignments set out in my law school texts I imagined I should be wearing a top hat and a swallow-tailed coat.

Mike Skerry, the clerk of the Malden Court, former Speaker of the Massachusetts Legislature, who had secured his appointment from an outgoing governor, and soon to become my best pal in the court, showed me these ropes.

"Look kid, I graduated from the sixth grade from Medford, and I could do one of these arraignments.

"First of all, everyone is mispronouncing the word. it's not 'a-rain-ment, It's arrangement."

Without a break, he continued with my third lesson at the Malden District Court University of Criminal Justice.

"Now look, first you come up to see me and give me one of these appearance notices. All you do is sign your name and fill in your address and phone number. Tell me when you want to come back to court, and I'll arrange it for you.

"Next you go over and see Teddy Fucillo, the assistant district attorney, or whichever of these bum cops who is handling the case. Make an arrangement with him for bail. Nine times out of ten he's gonna give you personal."

He drew the breath I was waiting for.

"When you're talking to the prosecutor, make arrangements to get the police reports. If you're not a fresh prick, he'll give them to you right away, or the next day."

"Finally, you gotta make an arrangement with your client to see him. Now, he's probably some fresh punk or a down in his luck poor slob, otherwise he'd be paying for his own lawyer. He's gonna want to see a lawyer like he wants to see a dentist. Try to see him in the courthouse. See him the same day if you can. Give him your business card. Nine times out of ten, he's gonna lose it, but give it to him anyway."

This last advice stung. I had just received a box of two hundred cards from the county. I had included the telephone number of my father's law office, without telling him or getting his permission. (I would straighten this out later). I never had a business card before in my life, and I was handing them out like they were ducats.

By Thursday I had observed several dozen defense lawyers engaged in their trade. Arraignments were a snap, and pleas were just a little more difficult:

First time marijuana: continued without a finding for six months, to be dismissed if there is further difficulty with the court;

Bad check? Thirty days to make full restitution, dismissed;

Drunk driving? First offense? Forty-five-day loss of license, and the twelve-week program;

Teenager drinking in public.

"Don't let me see you here again."

The plea process was just an addendum to Mike Skerry's

arrangement rule.

These were things that I knew I could do, being the quick study that I had become.

During my first week I wandered between the two trial sessions held on the second floor. There, the mysteries of the rules of evidence and constitutional procedure unfolded before me. Lawyers whose names I recognized appeared for their paying clients for cases for which an acquittal was the only acceptable outcome. I paid close attention to their smooth advocacy, and precise examination and cross-examination of witnesses. On the second floor there was decorum. I heard some of them argue case precedent which I had studied in law school. They were who I was going to become, and I was thrilled with this prospect and deeply proud of my choice.

I was going to follow all of the rules of Judge Glazer and Mike Skerry: get there on time, no foolishness, and don't be a fresh prick. Nuns at St Aidan's school in Brookline, Jesuits at Boston College High, and assistant deans at Georgetown University, had all tried without success to break me of tardiness, foolishness and freshness. I intended to give in to Judge Glazer. For a little while. There was nothing in that courthouse that bothered me, and I was loving every minute there.

My orientation was completed on Friday. I spent the weekend making sure my briefcase had enough yellow legal pads, pens, appearance slips, and a handbook on Massachusetts statutes. My wallet bulged with my business cards. All I needed was a shoeshine and a pressed two-piece suit.

On Monday I stepped into court, took a seat behind the defense table, waved to Freddie Agnetta the chief court officer, shot the breeze with the Medford and Everett cops, and waited for the little guy to enter the courtroom through a floor to ceiling velvet drape behind the judge's bench at precisely 9:00 a.m. He did not disappoint me.

The second arraignment of the day was mine. A teenager from Melrose was arrested during the weekend for drinking beer on the fairway of a local country club. He was seventeen, a senior at Melrose high and unemployed: He qualified for a public defender. I stepped up to the plate. In one continuous motion I gave my card to the indigent defendant, opened up my calendar, looked at the nearby probation officer who muttered "no record," and then addressed the court about releasing "my guy" on personal and setting up a trial date.

Glazer looked down at me with a pained expression on his face and motioned me to the sidebar.

I shrugged my shoulders with a "who me?" expression and went over to speak to him off the record.

"What's this foolishness?" he asked.

"What do you mean foolishness?" I responded.

"Why are you asking for a trial date?"

"Because I thought that's why I'm here" I replied.

"We don't try these cases. Speak to the Melrose Sergeant during the break. Talk to your client. Find out how much time he needs for paying a twenty-five-dollar fine, and we'll dismiss the case."

"But what happens if he's innocent and wants a trial?" I asked.

"Don't be foolish!" he ordered.

At the break I went into the hallway and learned that my client was thrilled to pay twenty-five dollars that day, and never see me or the court again.

Things picked up after the break. By the end of the day, I had four cases: two drunk drivings, a bad check client with a prior record, and a "b and e" in the daytime that would most likely be broken down to trespass. I would probably try one of the drunk driving cases, and while I was not yet prepared, I was certainly ready to do my best.

~

I crossed over Memorial Bridge. After twenty-eight years living in Boston, I was just discovering that the best view of the city was from across the Charles River in Cambridge. With the right sunlight, the golden dome of the statehouse set above the Beacon Hill townhouses and apartments, and against the office towers rising behind it, is the most picturesque scene in Boston. If everything went well this afternoon, I would get to see it every day.

I parked my car in the Government Center garage and walked over the hill to Bromfield Street. I had plans to see my father, Robert Muse, in his law office.

Bromfield runs between Tremont and Washington Streets in an area now known as Downtown Crossing. It is located a block up from the Park Street Church, which fronts the Boston Common.

At the head of the street is the Old Granary burial ground, the final resting place of such Boston Hall of Famers as Mother Goose, Samuel Adams and James Otis. At the other end was Filene's and its world famed Basement, marketplace for the masses, with suits and dresses discounted to unrealistically low prices. It was a great place for lunchtime browsing.

44 Bromfield St is a two elevator, nine story office building. The top floor is reachable only by stairs, and the former architect's loft was divided into five rooms and renamed the Penthouse. Robert F. Muse's law office occupied the Penthouse.

It was four o'clock, the approximate starting time for trial attorneys' second jobs. After mornings and early afternoons in court, most trial lawyers begin the work of returning phone calls, dictating letters, and reviewing case files. I walked into my father's office as he was opening up his mail.

His was the largest office on the floor. It was darkly stained wainscoted, cluttered with mismatched furniture---there was a psychiatrist couch and a Vermont maple rocking chair---and filled with file cabinets and boxes which overflowed with probably very important paper.

When I walked through the French doors which separated him from his secretary, he waved and voiced me a big but garbled hello. He had a recently lit cigar clenched between his teeth, and a phone in one hand, and a typed document in the other. His grunt and gesture signaled the familiar "Hi Chris…come in here." I knew this because once he understood he could not speak with the cigar in his mouth, he took it out and repeated, clearly "Hi Chris… come in here."

I took a seat in the rocking chair that faced his desk, with so many papers strewn on it that it constituted a fire trap. In fact, he would invariably state, as he placed a burning match at the end of his cigar, If this (the match) drops…poof,..what a malpractice case with all these files burned."

He leaned in his tan leather chair against the back wall whose nearly every available inch was covered by photographs, memorabilia, newspaper clippings and pages from documents that used to be important. He had pictures of all eleven of his children, several grandchildren, and my mother. In the middle of the wall was a photo of his Second World War Marine Corps fighter pilot squadron. He often insisted that he would have stayed in the

Pacific after the war if he knew his eight sons (not, no never, his three daughters) were in his future. He was only kidding: We all felt his love, and he was always a best buddy to each of us.

I gave him my career update. In the beginning he listened attentively to my enthusiastic description of my work and the go-ings-on in the Malden District court. I referenced some of the cops and lawyers that sent their hellos. I highlighted and exaggerated all of the little things that were new and different to me, and so very much routine to him. Finally, I broke the ice on the topic that was on my mind.

"I'll be doing most of my work at the courthouse. But the good news is I can also do private work, criminal, civil anything. Just as long as I take care of all the court appointed stuff first."

'That's a good deal," he said.

"So, as I see it, I need a mail drop, and a phone…"

Before I paused, he said, "Take the small office down the hall and have the secretary call and get a phone installed. Just don't screw up the files when you move them."

"That's great." I replied, first thinking, "I didn't expect the office," and then wondering "how could I ever screw up any of his files?"

I pressed on. At this point, (it usually happened after ten minutes), he began to act distracted. He puffed his cigar and started pulling his mail out of the envelopes.

"I get a monthly stipend of a thousand dollars from the County. It's a good start, but I'll need more for my expenses and everything. So, if you can, I'd like it if you could throw some work my way….anything…you know research…I'll do anything…I mean, I've got a lot to learn…."

He interrupted me as he pulled an official looking docu-ment from a large brown envelope. "Here's something." he said, "Rudy Pierce just appointed me to a Habeas Corpus case."

He paused and reviewed the documents for a minute.

"This is from a guy in Norfolk that's been convicted of murder…let's see, his name is Bobby Joe Leaster…this is his third time in Federal Court."

He lifted the papers to me with an underhanded thrust. "Here, go practice on this case. This is his third time...he sounds like a crybaby… work the case up, but look, make sure you go talk to him. I don't want you to just look at his file. Go talk to him."

I looked at the paperwork. I saw "United States District Court—petition for writ of Habeas Corpus—Bobby Joe Leaster, petitioner....petitioner's address: Massachusetts Correctional Institution, Norfolk."

"Murder...you want me to do a murder case?" I asked with hesitation and doubt.

"You can't do any worse than the lawyers who did his other appeals. Just make sure you go talk to him."

In a half hour I was standing at "The Littlest Bar" around the corner on Province Street. The "Littlest" was the smallest bar in Boston, measuring, on a good day, -when the licensing people were in a good mood- maybe 20 feet by 8. It had, as its front window advertised, *"ambiance."* I passed pleasantries with Gino the bartender and sipped a long neck bottle of Bud. The whole day was a rush: Things were looking up, and I was pretty full of myself. I had just finished my first full day on the job. I had my own office, and the promise of being able to do some extra paying work. My caseload was exploding: two drunk drivings, one bad check, one "B and E" and....one first degree murder.

"First degree murder" I said to myself. In the words of Mike Skerry, I felt "as nervous as a pregnant nun in a convent." I would be sure to follow Dad's advice and go visit my new client.

BOBBY JOE LEASTER

I was excited about meeting Chris Muse for the first time at Norfolk. I did not kill Levi Whiteside, and I did not rob his store. After the jury convicted me, I went straight to Walpole prison, and never saw a lawyer again, except for Bill Homans who took up my appeal, and he visited me just once. I filed two federal appeals, and got lawyers appointed. But they only wrote to me a few times, including telling me I lost again. This was my third federal habeus, and the court appointed Mr. Muse, Chris's dad to represent me. I can't describe how excited I was that a live lawyer would come to see me.

I was in Boston for just more than a year when they arrested me on a Sunday afternoon. I was going to start a new job on Monday. I was living in the South End with my girlfriend Judy. Living with a white girl like Judy was something I could never think of doing back in Reform, Alabama where I grew up.

When I was a kid, I seldom got into fights. I might argue a taste_or two with the guy I grew up with, but I never got into any bad fights or nothing. I was basically a very quiet kid growing up down south. I wasn't capable of doing anything like that because I wasn't raised like that. I wasn't raised in a way that you just go out and take from other folks: I mean, you know, take their money or their jewelry or whatever. And taking somebody else's life was out of the question for me, totally out of the question. It's just not in me to do that.

I was the baby in the family, so I got lots of love and attention, especially from my mother. And I was very close to my cousins, especially Earl, who had taken a bus to Boston. When he phoned, he talked about jobs and freedom and lots of pretty ladies. My other cousin Ruby had been calling me when I was in school to tell me Boston was a nice place to come. So, I decided to join Earl and Ruby right after graduation in the summer of 1969. I was eighteen years old, and I was just saying to myself I'm getting out of high school, now and I am a young man, and all I see ahead of me is my future leaving home, settling down somewhere, raising a family, and becoming a man. That's what my intention was when I came to Boston.

Booking photo, Boston Police Distric3, Dorchester MA, 9/27/70.

I got a job within days after the bus left me off in Boston. I

33

had money in my pocket and gave some to Ruby who took me in. I went downtown with Willie Earl, and just took in the freedom. I went to night clubs like the Sugar Shack and played basketball on the neighborhood courts. I met Judy, and she asked me to move in with her. Everything was great until I left the apartment to go get Judy a pack of cigarettes that day.

I was walking on Mass Ave next to St. Botolph Street, talking to my friend Pedro. A police wagon passed me then made a U-turn and stopped near us. A cop yelled, "Hey you," and I thought they were talking to Pedro. Then he said, "No not him, you. You are wanted for murder on Talbot Ave." They put me in a paddy wagon, and that's when my nightmare began.

COOLIDGE CORNER

I look back at my early years and see how cleverly my parents managed eleven children with boisterous personalities: They put us to work.

My older brothers, Michael and Robert, and I, (my father designated us the "first platoon") while still plodding along at St. Aidan's, found work at Pelham Drug Store two blocks from our home on Green St. From 3:00 to 6:00 pm we hopped on our bikes and delivered prescription drugs and sometimes, for the elderly, everything from shampoo to newspapers. We stayed busy, and mostly out of trouble, and we expanded our world to at least a radius of a mile from Coolidge Corner.

Coolidge Corner stands at the intersection of Beacon and Harvard Streets in Brookline. From Beacon Hill, through the Back Bay that was constructed with fill in the tidal flats of the Charles River in mid nineteenth century, through Brookline to the rustic Chestnut Hill, Beacon Street has been the favored migratory path of the very wealthy to escape the congestion and sometimes the blight of the downtown sections of Boston. Brookline people were called the *Wealthy Towners,* which was the team slogan for years at its high school. Veering left at the end of Beacon Street at Cleveland Circle, there is a road to one of the first private golf courses in the United States, called, *The* Country Club. Harvard and Yale Alumni who attended *The* Game in either Cambridge or New Haven could tee off with a round of golf at a very precious address. Beacon Street is a grand boulevard and a historic pathway for *The* very important people of old Boston.

Harvard Street was constructed with curves and in pieces. It joined Huntington Ave. and connected Roxbury to Alston and other parts of Brighton. There was a bus route from Dudley, now Nubian, Square to Union Square, that passed working class districts over Mission Hill, to the Jamaicaway, past St. Mary's church and the Irish enclave at Brookline Village, across Beacon Street, along a mile of Kosher shops and Temple Israel, to the commercial district of Union Square and the bus turnaround next to Twin Donuts. It had a different vibe.

For years, at the Beacon Street stop light, an old red-faced man we all knew simply as Moe, sold papers all day long from a bookcase- like newsstand with four or five shelves that held the different daily editions of the *Boston Globe* and the Record American. Moe was an amputee, and set his milk crate seat on Beacon Street, as it hugged the northbound Harvard Street across from the iconic S.S. Pierce building and turret, and in front of Liggett's Drug Store. Everyone suspected that Moe did more at that newsstand because every evening at 6:00 pm, after he counted out the papers and turned them over to the night shift, he was picked up in a late model Cadillac driven by a friend or maybe his wife. That is when I and the little Muses took over.

My family, without design, became a temporary labor supplier. We manned the newspaper deliveries for Leo Pelletier's distribution office in the back of his grocery store, stocking and delivery services for Larry Fishman at Pelham drug, and street hawkers at Tommy Ferris' newsstand. Jobs were passed down from Michael the oldest, to Jimmy, the youngest, who was just a year or two older than Oliver Twist, of London workhouse fame, when he began selling newspapers late into the night. The eight brothers were easily recognized for decades, and each was identified simply as "Musie."

While we were earning spending money, we were not getting into trouble. My parents were clever.

Sitting at Moe's milk crate those evenings as a fifteen-year-old kid, I got to see many things that got me thinking about matters different than hoping that a customer let me keep the two penny change from the sale of an 8-cent newspaper.

First, it was the swarm of customers who crowded around the newsstand every night. The *Globe* published its last, *Final*

Stocks, edition, and the coat-and-tie crowd, anxious for their investments, waited in line to check their daily scores.

Another crowd, with a few women, and working or casually clothed, clustered around me to buy the tabloid Record American. The object of their interest was the back page that had, incongruously, the daily parimutuel take at several racetracks across the country. For example, Santa Anita may have reported $125,651 and two other racetracks posted their end of the day betting receipts. The last number for each track, in order of position gave the three-digit *Number* that identified the winner of an illegal lottery that was held in every city across the country. These folks had bet dimes to a dollar on the Daily Number and stood in line with hope. A one-dollar bet produced $600.00 in winnings, half the price of a cheap new car. A dime, successfully bet, netted $60.00, a week's wages for some.

So, my first fifteen minutes was spent tending to the two groups of gamblers of different economic and social class. My memory is that the daily number crowd gave me the two cents change from the dime they used to buy the Record, and the *Globe* and stocks crowd waited for their change. I learned you got rich by counting your pennies. I also learned to tip, or actually over tip, when I got older and spent money freely.

My ten- and eleven-year-old brothers, "little Musies," would start their days at St. Aidan with the nuns asking, "Who made you?" and ten hours later answering men pulling next to the newsstand shouting, "Hey kid. What's the number?"

Then there was one guy who not only did not tip but stole one paper and tried a few more times. He was a mouthy downtown lawyer who drove a big Lincoln Continental up beside me and yelled for me to bring him a *Globe*. I went to him. He asked if I "was a Muse." He told me his name, and said he knew my father. Then he flashed a hundred-dollar bill in my face. That's all he had. Could I give him the change?
"Too bad, I'll pay you tomorrow," as he sped off.

I was out 8 cents and a boatload of pride. I told my father about this, and he quickly identified the "thief." A few days later, Bob saw the attorney who thought he could embarrass him in front of some other lawyers.

"I saw your kid selling papers. Things that bad?"

"Not bad at all. You still using that hundred-dollar trick?

You stiffed him, you cheap bastard."

After the swarm left there was often a sad looking woman who remained. I learned early on that the number stenciled on her arm signaled that she was a Holocaust survivor, who lost her entire family to Hitler, a Christian's, purge. Her face was worn out with wrinkles, rough and blotchy. Her hair was grey, singed, and scraggly. Her clothing was dated and the same every day I saw her. Often loud, sometimes with a whisper, she would still scream to anyone and everyone, and sometimes to no one:

"God damned Jesus. Jesus Christ, Go to hell. If God is dead, God is in hell."

When I saw her, I could not wait for the seven o'clock hour when she would disappear into the night. I was a fifteen-year-old kid who had difficulty processing something I remembered for the rest of my life. Unsettling things are often best, or maybe just easily, avoided.

Every once in a while, I would hear a siren and see blue lights behind a car on Harvard Street coming towards me. The car would pull over at the stoplight, and the Brookline policeman would approach the driver's window. Sometimes the driver and other occupants were directed out of the car. Usually after a conversation, everyone returned to their automobiles and drove away. Usually, almost always, the driver was Black. Brookline enjoyed a very low crime rate. I don't recall anyone who managed the town finding objection with this, a customary and tolerated police procedure. What was routine for them was normal for me: Just sirens and blue lights that sometimes broke up my night.

Green Street was perpendicular to Harvard St. Walking to the newsstand, for a period of several weeks, I observed crowds of Black men and women marching with picket signs in front of our local Woolworth's five and ten, a few stores down from Brigham's Ice Cream Shop in the Alston direction. It was at a time when there were sit-ins at Woolworths in the deep South. I saw the demonstrations on television, but I did not connect what was happening in Brookline with them. Heck, everyone could eat at the Coolidge Corner branch.

I had a similar reaction to the pickets that walked in a circle in front of Liggett's Drug Store, protesting the real estate brokers who had offices above it on the second floor. I forget what was exactly printed on their placards, except the words 'rental' and "discrimination" have stuck in my memory. I was fifteen. I guess I knew what they were protesting: I knew there was something wrong going on, but I cannot say it very much concerned me.

My parents were very clever. They put us to work to earn some spending money and to stay out of trouble, and I think now, to let us see a world that was close to our doorstep, but far away from our lives. Learning that there were those who lived lives different from mine was a lesson my parents taught without a lecture, sometimes with commentary, and I think, with early and lasting effect.

We went to different schools, together (1962-63).

Fifth Grade B

These boys and girls are active and curious about Science around them. They observe, listen, think, tell, ask, experiment learn. Mrs. J. L. Lark, Instructor

Chapter Two

THE CASE

The notice of appointment of counsel from the Federal Court contained the petition for Writ of Habeas Corpus. Attached to it was a copy of the 1972 Supreme Judicial Court decision which upheld the murder conviction. This satisfied the procedural requirement that the petitioner had exhausted all available state remedies before filing for Federal Court review. More importantly, Commonwealth vs. Bobby Joe Leaster gave me the short, abbreviated version of the trial, and reading it was the first step of a ten-year journey.

On September 27, 1970, two Black males, one armed with a long barrel .22 caliber pistol, robbed and assaulted Levi Whiteside, and his wife Kathleen, at the Talbot variety store in the Dorchester section of Boston.

Levi, the store owner went to the assistance of his wife as one of the robbers held a gun to her head and demanded money. During a struggle, Levi was shot. Within minutes police arrived and a description of the robbers was broadcast over police airwaves. Meanwhile Levi was rushed by ambulance to Boston City Hospital where he was pronounced dead several minutes after his arrival.

Around 5:15 p.m. Bobby Joe was arrested in the South End by police officers on patrol who had heard the description on the police radio. Leaster's clothing matched that of the shooter. At approximately 5:30 p.m. Bobby Joe was transported in a **wagon** to the parking area fronting the emergency room of City Hospital. He was taken from the wagon in handcuffs, escorted by uniformed police officers to a cruiser, just as Kathleen was leaving the emergency room with a sergeant. Mrs. Whiteside saw Bobby Joe as he was walking. She asked if she could take a closer look at the man who looked like the one who killed her husband. The sergeant walked her to the window of the cruiser where Bobby Joe was now seated in the back seat. There she identified him based in part on the dark bruise- like birthmark below his left eye.

These facts got my interest. From law school I knew that there was something wrong with this ID process. I felt some comfort in the realization that I could, at least in the academic sense, handle the obvious issue. Suggestive police line-ups, photo arrays, and like here, show-ups were usually improper, and often unconstitutional. The logic in excluding from evidence these kinds of identifications is obvious: the police have all but put a sign around the suspect's neck saying, "He's the guy." Misidentifications often occur because the victim or witness is tacitly asked to agree with the cops.

There are exceptions to the ordinary rule in favor of exclusion. The Supreme Court has carved out the "exigent circumstance" rule. The police may bring a suspect to the bedside of a dying witness, without making a lawyer available, and conduct a suggestive confrontation. Its rationale is obvious: the victim probably knows the killer, and his time to say so was running out. I recalled the case of <u>Stovall vs. Denno</u> from my Constitutional law studies. In the Leaster case, the state supreme court adopted this reasoning and ruled:

> "The judge found as a matter of fact 'based upon pure inference' the reason Frost (the arresting police officer) was told to take the suspect (defendant) to the Boston City Hospital was in order to arrange a face-to-face confrontation with the victim, Levi Whiteside; that neither Frost nor police headquarters knew Levi was dead, and that the confrontation in the parking lot was not 'prearranged'. The police had no plans for a confrontation or identification of the suspect by Mrs. Whiteside."

As I read that neither Frost not Headquarters knew that Levi was dead, I momentarily flashed back to my first-year law school classroom when the Criminal Law instructor gave an energized description of *causation*. He gave the example of the defendant who shot a guy and wounded him, who is in an ambulance and while driven to the hospital is in a bad accident and dies. Is defendant guilty of murder?

My friend Jim Norton, a probation officer at the Roxbury District Court who had seen dozens of murder arraignments, whispered to me, "No one in Boston dies at the scene, it's always at City Hospital.

"Huh? Why?"

"Because you can't move a dead body until the medical examiner arrives to declare the guy dead. No cop wants to stick around a stinkin' corpse until they get the ME off the golf course."

My other unfiltered moment brought me back to my high school years when I worked part time at City Hospital. The back door opened to Albany Street where you could look up the street to the Emergency Room entrance and parking area, and down the street to the city morgue. I could visualize the activity described in the decision, and I was haunted by what Jim said a few years back. There were hospital emergency rooms closer to Talbot Ave., but none were closer to a morgue.

I returned to the case and saw, predictably, that the court denied his appeal on the grounds of an unconstitutional show-up. It also denied Bobby Joe's challenges to jury instructions and to other evidence issues.

The decision contained the names of the trial and appellate counsel, Charles Lewis and William Homans.

I knew Mr. Homans well by reputation, and slightly from an introduction by my father. I wrote him a letter, advised him of my co-counsel role, and asked to review and copy the file. I also wrote to Bobby Joe at Norfolk prison and told him that my father was appointed to represent him, that I would assist him, and that after I had assembled his trial record, I would visit him.

Mr. Homans' office was in the renovated Old City Hall which also housed Maison Robert, the best outdoor café in Boston. The previous May, I'd celebrated my passing the bar exam there, at a table under the shadow of an oversized statue of Ben Franklin, with $500 worth of chilled white, perfect for a spring afternoon - Pouilly Fuisse wine – to be precise, 40 bottles, on Bob Muse's Mastercard and a steady stream of congratulations from family and friends who dropped by. Homans' office was more cluttered than my father's and I concluded that all trial lawyers were slobs. I became such a slob, and I suppose these early experiences were the source of my flawed organizational habits.

I spoke with Mr. Homans for at least an hour. He welcomed me to the case and advised me that this was one of the two most troubling in his career. He recalled how Bobby's lawyer, Charles Lewis, reached out to him soon after the verdict, distraught at the outcome, and enlisted him to complete and argue the Leaster appeal. I walked away with two full armloads of paperwork that Mr. Homans carried on his failed journey to the Supreme Judicial Court. I smugly thought I was going to fix that blatant miscarriage of justice—quickly and easily—with the help of the Federal Court.

WALPOLE

I remember the day the judge sentenced me to Walpole like it was yesterday. The correction officers handcuffed me and took me down an elevator to the back of the Suffolk Courthouse. They drove a Ford. They both had short sleeved shirts because it was summer.

At the traffic lights the driver turned left on Cambridge Street going to Mass General. I wasn't paying attention to where they were driving.

He got on the ramp to Storrow Drive. I don't remember ever being on that road before. But they drove along the Charles River which I knew. Then he drove to Kenmore Square, which I knew, and around Fenway Park, which I had seen but never went into.

Everything else was a blur, even though I stared out the window at houses and traffic. About an hour later I saw a sign which said Walpole Center. I remember this because the driver turned to me and said, You're almost home."

I saw the word "Walpole" on signs everywhere, like town hall and a police station. This woke me right up.

"Walpole?" I thought to myself . That's what the judge said when he sentenced me for life to Walpole State Prison. In a few miles I saw this big gray, at least twenty-foot wall next to me. The car turned into this long driveway. It was just starting to get dark. The officers opened the door and told me to get out. They took off the chains and pushed me to an office. The officer, the fat one, said "He's a lifer...first degree murder." He handed over a paper and both of them left me.

After one guy did some paperwork, they walked me down a long hall. They put me in a room and told me to take off my clothes. A guard looked into my mouth with a small flashlight, then told me to bend over and he shined the light into my hole. Then they put me in a shower room, and then gave me a shirt and pants that were like hospital clothes. A few minutes later they marched me down another hallway to a metal door which he opened and told me, "This is your new home. Behave yourself and the rest of your life will be nicer." I didn't know that this was a temporary cell. It had no light in it. I remembered my whole day in court. I told the jury "I never hurt anybody, never killed anyone in my life. I never saw that place in my whole life." Then after they came back and said I was guilty, the Judge said, "Bobby Joe Leaster, I sentence you for life to Walpole State Prison." I thought I had to spend the rest of my life in that dark cell. So, there was no one else around, and I just started crying and called out for my momma.

~

My first days at Walpole were hell. After a few days I was put in general population with 800 prisoners who were the worst in the system. I was scared to death. I was all alone I was shy. I kept to myself. I cried to myself every night.

But I always had to have my faith in God. You always have to have faith in God. Don't ever lose faith. God will always make a way for your life. My God told me, "My hand will be on you. I am going to watch over. Make sure you survive."

In the first days I met two inmates who helped me. Both doing life for murder. I still talked like I was from the country. They said that to me. They knew I wasn't a murderer, just looking at me. They told me they heard about my murder case. I told them I was innocent and would be out in a few months once my lawyers started working on it. They laughed. "We've been here for eight years, probably be here for another twenty. Once you are guilty, you need to appeal It takes a long time. You aren't going any place. We'll show you the ropes."

They put me in a single cell. They have 3 or 4 tiers of cells and are locked at night. They open up in the morning to go to breakfast, then you go to your jobs. I went to the plate shop to make license plates. I also worked in the kitchen. One day the guard told me I was assigned to the laundry. "Guess who you will be working with?" He told me Albert DeSalvo, like he was a celebrity or something. I didn't know him. The guard told me, "Don't you know, he's the Boston Strangler!" I was not excited.

After lunch you go back to your cell for a count. They stay locked until they yell YARD, and then you can go to the yard to lift weights or shoot baskets. I played 3 on 3. You play until you lose. I was good and stayed on the court a lot.

I didn't have many visitors. Judy came a few times. My nephew Earl came but it was hard to get there. So, I was basically all alone. In five months, I got classified to go to Norfolk a few miles down the road. My life became a whole lot better. We had rooms, not cells. You could fix them up with pictures and stuff like that. We could have food and things sent to us. Earl bought me a TV. The room had a radio. They put 50 guys in a unit, you had a common area and a bathroom. Doors were not locked except the door into the unit.

I got jobs in the tailor shop and the laundry. I worked with Paul McKenzie and Frank Brimage. We were paid like 25 cents a day. I got paid every three months I could use it to buy things in the commissary. Earl put more money in my account, but it was not much because he had little kids now.

I played a lot of basketball because mentally it eased the pain. There was an outdoor court at Cadillac Alley. It was a made-up name. Inmates would gather there and brag about how much money they made before robbing and selling drugs, and about their Cadillacs.

One day I was playing at Cadillac Alley, and I got into a fight with another inmate because he made an insult about my mother. It was just shoving, and it was broken up and we went back to playing. When the game finished, I ran back to the dorm area. When I turned a corner, the other inmate stepped out behind me and stabbed me three times with a shiv. That's what we call spoons and combs and things that could be sharpened until they became knives.

I was on the ground bleeding: I was losing consciousness. A guard stood over me and said "This young man is hurt. He probably won't make it." I'm on the ground asking God, "Did I do something wrong? Is this the end of my life, 24 years old, dead in prison? Is that your plan? Take me if you must, but why God?"

They took me to Norwood Hospital where I stayed for 6 nights. I told the guards that I must have backed into a nail. I did not snitch. Inmates were getting stabbed constantly. If you snitched you would get badly punished. I didn't have problems with anyone, even with the guy that stabbed me, because I didn't snitch on him.

I didn't have many visits. Judy went to New Orleans and married my friend Jack Clay. Earl came when he could. My mother came once. But she got all upset that I didn't want her to have that pain. So, I asked her not to return. My dad never came.

SEEING A LAWYER'S FACE

Soon after receipt of my letter, Bobby Joe called me,

collect, from prison. I had already recruited a law student to assist in the research. Billy Kennedy was in my office when I received this call. I told Bobby that I would see him in the next several weeks. I asked him if he would be available for a certain day. He agreed, and I penciled the date in my calendar. When I got off the phone, Billy all but called me an idiot.

"Where do you think he was going to be. He's doing a life sentence. What do you mean, "Are you available? Where's he gonna be? Nantucket?"

I drove to Norfolk prison on the designated afternoon. Norfolk is 2 or 3 miles from Walpole prison, this was my first time in a state prison. The whole setting −the walls, the barbed wire, the guards, the security checkpoint− is extremely intimidating to the first-time visitor. I filled in the information form, emptied my pockets of all valuables, and went through the metal detectors. My name was called, and I was directed through a succession of metal doors. I entered through one, waited for the door behind me to close, then waited for the one in front of me to open. It was claustrophobic. Once through the gauntlet, I was met by a guard and brought to an attorney conference room. I can still recall the staleness of the air inside that section of the prison.

Bobby Joe entered the room accompanied by another inmate, whom I readily understood to be the jail house lawyer who helped file Bobby's petition.

"Victor" outlined the issues he considered to be worthwhile. He quoted decisions from Federal Courts throughout the country. He spoke of judges with both first and last names, as if he went to bar association dinners with them. He distinguished the Fifth from the Ninth Circuit, and advised me which cases to look at, and others to ignore. Victor left me with the feeling that if I practiced for five more years and paid close attention, I could become his equal. I hadn't a clue what he was talking about, but it sounded impressive.

I interviewed Bobby from a client intake form I used in the Malden court.

He was one of nine children who was raised by both parents in rural Alabama, in a town called Reform. I made sure 'Reform' was correctly stated: It was, and I moved beyond the irony. He came to Boston soon after his high school graduation in 1969. He had been working at the time of the murder, and he had no prior criminal record. Although I only had a month of work under my belt at Malden Court, it seemed that every single one of my clients: (a) came from a broken home (b) quit school at sixteen or earlier, (c) was unemployed, and (d) had a prior record. Bobby Joe had not even been arrested before.

I completed the background part of the interview, loosened my tie, sat up straight, and began my sales pitch. I told Bobby that we would be happy to handle his appeal. We were eminently qualified, what with my extensive background as a public criminal defender, and my father's reputation as one of the best trial lawyers in town. Victor nodded approvingly, letting me know he had heard of Robert Muse. (and probably attended lawyer conferences with him). I told Bobby that he did not have to worry about paying us, and that the Federal Court would subsidize his legal fees. ($750 was allocated for this kind of appeal, which we never billed).

When Bobby agreed to become my client, I was not aware that I was the first lawyer he had seen face to face since Bill Homans finished his state appeal. I learned later that just two months before our meeting, he received a letter stating that "after careful review" attorneys from a prisoner rights project "have concluded that there are no issues which could serve as a basis for a Federal Habeas Corpus petition." There was a reason he treated *My Cousin Vinny 's* alter ego like Clarence Darrow.

We went over the general parameters of the charges and the trial. Bobby told me insistently that he was innocent. There was no place in my form to check off "innocent" or "guilty." In correct criminal defender protocol, I was prepared to represent him even if he was guilty. It was my absolute naivete and inexperience that caused me to conclude that he was innocent; otherwise, why would he constantly claim it?

When I drove home, I had a pit in my stomach. "Here's a guy who did not just receive a fair trial....he's innocent" I thought. I never challenged this belief.

Before I finished, I looked at the jail house lawyer, and asked if he too was set up, was he also an innocent man? Why was he in Norfolk?

He burst out laughing. He told me he was in Norfolk fair and square for securities fraud. He was what some people call, a con man.

The next day I told my father about my visit.

"I think he's innocent. The identification procedure was worthless, and it screwed him. It should not have been admitted."

Our senior counsel was skeptical. "Everyone in prison says he is innocent."

"But this guy really is. I can feel it. Look, I will get going with research on the admissibility of accidental suggestive identifications, but you have to go see him."

He relented and promised to go visit our new client in the next few days.

BIG BOB

My son CJ gave my father the name Big Bob, or Big as he called him. It fit him perfectly, as I knew no person who constantly had so many big ideas, or bigger ways of doing things.

He came from humble beginnings in Stoneham MA, a depression boy, he called himself.

His French-Canadian father was a laborer, like his father who came south from Nova Scotia and his grandfather before him. His neighborhood in Stoneham was called Dogtown, populated with Italians, Irish, and Jews, all poor like himself. His mother was a McHale, with old fashioned attachments to parish churches and schools. He had no option to attend public school. "Big" attended St. Patrick's under the pain of mortal sin. The only Boy Scout troop in town met in a Congregational church, and special permission was required to join. To say that Catholics and Protestants were antagonistic to each other understates their history in eastern Massachusetts. It is sort of like saying "Red Sox fans really don't like the Yankees."

I believe Ma, as we called her, made sure her number one son went further than St. Patrick's grammar school, and onto a college path. Irish are known for four things; happy war ballads, sad love melodies, Catholic faith, and education. Ma was going to make sure her Bobby was going to be more Irish than French when it came to education. His next stop was Malden Catholic High School.

Looking back, "Big" would recall with fondness his four years at MC. He developed lifetime friendships, became expert at debate and at least functional on the hockey rink. Most importantly, he became the first member of his family to attend college. It was, predictably, Boston College, as BC was the destination of most Catholic students in greater Boston. Even if you were smart and could afford it, the Catholic boy was unlikely to attend Harvard and lose his faith.

Boston College gave my father his exit from Dogtown. It was the ebbtide of the depression, and his Uncle Arthur bought him a car to drive the fifteen miles to the *Heights* each day. He made some of the greatest friends in his life, and their collective stories spoke of the fun they all had until, as my mother described December 1941: "Then came Pearl Harbor and everything changed."

My mother grew up on the fringe of the Boston College campus. She was born in a beautiful brick house that later became the rectory for St. Ignatius Church, as close to a Jesuit cathedral as there is in Boston. Her parents sold it to the Jesuits, who moved the house a short distance then built the church on the enlarged lot. The forward part, the sanctuary, sits where my mother was physically born. When she passed away at 94, her funeral, like my father's, was at St. Ignatius, and her casket was placed in the same spot as her birth. She is buried with my father in the cemetery directly across the street from the church.

When her house was sold, during and because of the great depression, my mother moved across Commonwealth Avenue, a few blocks down from the church and the campus entrance. She attended Girls Latin School, and then Emmanuel College in the Fenway part of Boston. She commuted and lived with her mother, a physician, and her father, an Irish immigrant builder. Dr. Beatty's parents emigrated from Ireland, and she became one of the first women graduates of Tufts Medical School before entering the medical and civic world of Boston like an explosion. She became the superintendent of the Mattapan Sanatorium that cared for thousands during the tuberculosis epidemic that strangled much of our country. Mayor James Michael Curley appointed her, the first woman, to a coveted and powerful position of trustee of Boston City Hospital.

It was there on an early summer day in 1940 that Mary Beatty saw my father trekking through campus on his way to class, a summer school makeup course for the Latin that he had earlier failed. Big Bob's favorite quote, which I often repeat, is that

"Success is failure turned inside out." I use it for more aspirational circumstances, as he often did. But his failure of Latin begat this obvious unintended success. He was smitten. They dated. They fell in love.

And then came Pearl Harbor.

The spring following that *day of infamy,* they both boarded a train at South Station. He was headed to Chapel Hill for Marine Corps flight training. She got off in Springfield and continued to Northampton where she joined the first class of Navy Waves. They did not see each other for 14 months when they had a hurried last-minute wedding and then were separated until my father's return from Okinawa.

"Moonie" as my son CJ renamed her, outranked my father as a First Lieutenant. After the war she was one of three women to enroll in Boston College Law School, paid for by the G I Bill.

She ended her legal career as a highly regarded Justice of the Suffolk County Probate Court, and an icon for the many women entering the profession. When she received a lifetime achievement award from B C Law, responding to a question of being a woman in an otherwise all male class, she told the audience that she had little concern: "I was used to giving orders to men during the war. Nothing would change in law school."

Wedding day, May 20, 1944, and a return to service.

The term, *Greatest Generation* while often overused,

captures the essence of World War ll returning veterans. My parents, like the millions of other enlistees, were babies, well at least just kids, when they journeyed to the inferno of war. When they returned as *Men* and as *Women*, all grown up beyond their years, surviving the indescribable, bearing witness to the death of friends, and living with the loss of family, there was very little that would deter them or throw them off course for the rest of the gift that was their future lives. After the war, no challenge was too great.

Big Bob was part of that generation. I am certain that speaking with Bobby Joe for the first time in Norfolk prison, becoming convinced of his innocence and making up his mind that he would correct that injustice, he knew that he was absolutely going to make it happen. The task was daunting, but he had worked through much tougher challenges flying Corsairs in the Pacific.

Chapter Three

LIKE SON, LIKE FATHER

Just like Chris promised, Mr. Muse came to see me at Norfolk. He saw me in the visitor room. He had a blue suit, a white shirt, a tie, and he wore a black overcoat, and a hat. He had a great smile on his face. He called me Bobby, not Bobby Joe.

He greeted me. He didn't just shake hands. He hugged me and everything. For the rest of my time in prison, for the rest of my life, to this day, I felt he was a second father to me.

Just like Chris, Mr. Muse took notes and asked me about my background, and my time in Boston.

When I got off the Greyhound, I was met by my Cousin Ruby Thomas and her sisters Inez and Pauline. Boston was the biggest city I had ever seen. I was amazed. It went on for miles and I was very excited about it My cousins took me in. I went first with Inez to Cleaves Road in Roxbury. I stayed close to her home because I didn't want to get lost. I walked around Franklin Field because it was easy to find my way home. In a month or so I got my first job at the Boston Sausage company over by the expressway near South Boston. I started paying my cousin $20.00 a week for rent.

Then in September I moved in with Pauline at Columbia Road, until February, when I went to Gladys' house on Geneva Ave.

The Sausage company shut down, so I got a job at the Sheraton in the Back Bay. I was a short order cook, mostly frying things. My mother taught me how to cook.

I used to go downtown to clubs with Earl and Jimmy Johnson, and one night at the Sugar Shack, I met Judy. I think that is when I quit my job at the Sheraton and went to a training program for General Dynamics, they had on Washington Street in Dorchester. I moved in with Judy that summer in the South End. Until then I never lived in a place with White people. It was fun and different. Then a few months later I got arrested.

I was shocked how Blacks and Whites were together in Boston, how Blacks owned businesses, even how Whites worked for Blacks.

Was Boston different from down south?

Whites would smile and be nice but behind your back they'd call you the "N" word. Down South they would say it to your face. But most of the time I felt welcome. Then again I stayed mostly in all Black neighborhoods in Boston. But the police were racist.

Who was racist? The person or the system?

Both. The arresting officer, Alton Frost, he just looked racist when he arrested me. He reminded me of people back home. When he said, 'Hey you' he sounded like back in the South when they would yell "Hey Boy." When the police went to Judy's house because I told them I was with her, they went into the kitchen looking for things, like drugs. He asked her, 'What are you doing with the "N"word? So, she told them she had not seen me since Friday, because the police would not tell her why they were looking for me. They did not tell her I was arrested. She was going to wait until I got home for me to tell her.

The system was racist. I just got to Boston and the police see this young Black man fresh from Alabama, and say let's get this guy, no one knows him anyway. They didn't investigate that crime at all. They got me one hour after the robbery. No investigation. They seen the opportunity to pin it on a Black guy. And the way the law was back then, they could do it. They would not let that murder go unsolved. They knew I was gullible about the law.

James Baldwin observed the scenery in America and its justice system at the same time Bobby Joe was living it, in a way he described in *No Name In The Street* (1972), which confirmed Bobby Joe's take on it:

"Well, if one really wishes to know how justice is administered in a country,….

Ask any Mexican, any Puerto Rican, any Black man, any poor person – ask the wretched how they fare in the halls of justice, and then you will know, not whether or not the country is just, but whether or not it has any love of justice, or any concept of it."

BOSTON, 1975, BUSING

I was in my second-year teaching at the Lewis Middle School in Roxbury when I was offered the public defender job. I had transferred to Lewis from a two- year position at East Boston

High School because the Federal Court busing order mandated more diversity in the classrooms, and that required more minority hires. I had an upfront look at one of the most explosive times in Boston's history.

I grew up in a Boston that was a racially segregated city. It was a segregation that was nearly indistinguishable from the apartheid of the South in its effect, although not with their laws. The White homeowner would claim that he did not create the racially divided city: He simply lived in it. Politicians had a quick and rote response that some schools were nearly all Black because the neighborhoods were that way.

Apologists would point out that Boston did not have any laws, like the Jim Crow ones, that ordered segregation. But the quickly ignored fact was that Black neighborhoods did not develop with the same forces of migration and settlement as those of their White neighbors: It was not that benign. Banks redlined areas where they would lend money for home mortgages. Realtors directed people of color away from White neighborhoods. And of course, in the absence of fair housing laws, landlords declined to rent. In Boston, and most major Northern cities, access to employment, quality housing, and education was not equal, and that was due to the politics of the city, and the attitudes of its citizens.

In my second year of law school, the first year of busing, I read the federal court decision that described how and why the Boston schools were systematically racially segregated. This finding stood behind the hundreds of pages of orders implementing the wholesale reorganization, and some might claim, demolition of the Boston Public schools.

This was not the first time the City of Boston was accused of racially assigning its students. In 1850 an African American, Benjamin Roberts, lived in Boston's North End. He refused to send his five-year-old daughter Sarah to the all-Black Abiel Smith school on the northside of Beacon Hill, a large populated and vibrant community of Black "freedmen" who provided service to the rich and the mighty, the *Brahmins*, of the top and south side of Beacon Hill. Sarah walked by two schools on the way to Abiel Smith. Benjamin claimed Abiel Smith was inferior to the White schools she passed, that the distance to travel was a burden, and that the racial segregation caused psychological harm. The School Committee determined that the policy "is not only legal and just but is best adapted to promote the education of that class of our population."

Robert Morris, the second African American lawyer in the United States, and one of Boston's finest, although least known, trial attorneys took up Sarah's case. Along with the abolitionist lawyer and future Senator, Charles Sumner, he filed suit and then an appeal.

The Law sometimes seems to follow algorithms, often ignoring justice. This was such a case. Lemuel Shaw, the Chief Justice of the Massachusetts' highest court focused on the school committee's assignment authority and found its decision to educate Black students separate from Whites was an administrative decision worthy of deference. Since little Sarah had access to a school *"as well conducted in all respects, and as well fitted, in point of capacity and qualification of the instructors, to advance the education of children under seven years old, as the other primary schools"* there was no violation of her rights. In other words, "separate but equal" was constitutional. It took a hundred years to reverse that awful legal phrase.

In a way, it was the reasoning of Chief Justice Shaw - deference to the school authorities- that gave cover to the Boston School Committee to create a dual system where Black neighborhood elementary schools fed its students to certain high schools, which in turn became all or nearly all Black. It was not done on the basis of race, they explained, perhaps with a wink and a nod: The enrollments evolved based on neighborhoods which were largely one race or the other, a demographic matter beyond the control of the committee. The elementary schools were built decades before to serve the local neighborhood populations, within walking distance to their homes. That the schools became racially imbalanced, in violation of a recently enacted statute, was not caused by the committee or its administrators, they argued.

Reasons would be offered, excuses were made, but the inescapable statistical fact was that the schools in Boston were racially segregated. This was the seventies: The battles in Selma and Little Rock had been fought; President Johnson's Civil Rights legislation was passed; Martin Luther King Jr. had been mourned and buried. There was no lack of either legal or moral direction. The destination was obvious, but the path was unclear. Worse, there was no leadership.

The contest in the federal courtroom was actually a brawl between the stubborn politicians who fueled their constituents with dissent and sometimes hate, or perhaps, simply reflected their dissent and hate, but never delivered compromise or settlement. Instead, by default, they gave that task to a federal judge, who knew how to dissect a case, and write a decision with clarity, correct on the law and the United States Constitution, but which fell short on providing an adequate and balanced educational remedy. In his decision, Judge Arthur Garrity found that the Boston School Committee *intended* that the system would become segregated because they, the committee, took actions which foreseeably, that is 'it was certain or substantially certain,' segregation would occur. His remedy, court ordered busing, transfers of teachers, and redrawing school lines, was problematic, and by some accounts, destructive and punitive. I stand with those who saw other, less destructive remedies available. However, no discussion of it in these pages would be helpful. What is relevant is the busing pre-history and aftermath.

And so, those videos of yellow school buses with small Black kids staring with terror in their eyes at White people throwing rocks and calling them the n-word, is now part of the permanent history of Boston. Those pictures are worth thousands of words, but they do not depict the whole story of the chaos, challenges, and the presence and absence of courage that also existed during a decade of unrest.

Common Ground by J. Anthony Lukas is the most comprehensive and best written account of the Boston Busing Era, which the author chronicled through the lives of three families who were impacted by the Federal Court. He viewed the conduct of broad swarths of the neighborhood populations with equal measure of criticism and sensitivity.

Those photos and videos that seem to appear in every made- in- Boston crime movie, never include the actions of the large percentage of the parents and students who had legitimate objections to the court order, the ones who refused to send their kids from one overcrowded underperforming school cross town to another low performing physically dated school just a few miles, but a world apart from their homes.

I taught those kids in schools in, respectively, nearly all Black and also, all White neighborhoods. My viewpoint may be found to be simplistic, although I believe accurate, it in no way excuses the vitriol and hate that surfaced during those turbulent days.

Wanting their kids to go to schools in their communities was not a novel idea. Words like familiarity, safety, convenience, and quality are easily interspersed in reasons given for choosing schools. Today, and then, when young parents search for their first home to purchase, their primary concern after cost, is where and how good are the schools. Can they walk their kids to school? Are they bussed more than a short distance? They trusted the familiarity of the neighborhoods to provide security and comfort to their kids. They valued the continuity of instruction from teachers who taught their older kids, and maybe the parents. Boston parents with kids assigned by the bussing orders expressed these feelings when they angrily asserted that the abutting towns, Brookline, Newton, Milton, and a few others, kept and treasured those benefits. The hypocrisy of busing proponents from the suburbs was palpable.

In the sixties and early seventies Boston neighborhoods operated like City States; the modern terminology is "cultural silos." Many residents had no reason to leave the neighborhood except for work. High school sports bound the neighborhoods. My BC High teams played in the City League with, Eastie, Southie, Dot, Chucktown (Tr: East Boston, South Boston, Dorchester, Charlestown) and other neighborhood high schools, which had huge followings at their games. Booster clubs supported them. Sometimes multiple generations of families attended the same school, and played the same sports. There was as much legacy interest there as places like Choate and Exeter Academies. There were legitimate, non-racist, reasons for objecting to or refusing to send their kids to schools outside of their self-contained communities.

To borrow the words of the Judge, it was foreseeable, "that it was certain or substantially certain," that these parents would react strongly against having a computer select the school assignments of their kids. Unfortunately, the parents had to choose sides which were color coded. And in too many instances, their objections became resentments and then hateful and then racist.

It was also foreseeable, "that is it was certain or substantially certain," that parents would vote with their feet. Large numbers put their kids in parochial schools, sent them to live with relatives in the suburbs, moved out of the city, or watched as their kids dropped out of school rather than move to one they did not choose. The reasons for doing so were often driven by racial animus, for sure, but for some, it was doing what they thought was best for their kids. The result was that the schools lost enrollments and became further segregated.

It was foreseeable that teacher and program quality would be impacted.

I was part of the teacher reassignment order of the federal court. The judge correctly found that Blacks were underrepresented in the teacher ranks, and that their absence among the Black students had obvious negative effect: *Were only Whites able to teach? Where were the Black role models?* So, while I agree that this situation needed a remedy without delay, and the active nationwide recruitment of Black teachers was an appropriate response, the implementation of the order came with predictable difficulty.

During the summer of 1975 I received notice that I was to be moved out of East Boston High, to a school to be determined in accordance with seniority. I went to a school in Dorchester where a bidding auction took place. All of the vacancies, mostly in the nearly all Black schools, were listed according to subject area. Another list of teachers in those subjects, was arranged according to seniority. As the day wore on, and most of the assignments were called out, I was left with two options. I chose the Lewis Middle School in Roxbury for no other reason than the Principal, Tom Mullin, came over to me and said, "Come on with us, kid, you'll love it." Now it was not a bad reason, and I did come to love it, but this definitely did not follow the "Queensbury Rules," or as it is now called, "Best Practices," of teacher recruitment and hiring the candidate who "was the right fit."

In my Commercial Code class in law school, I learned the term *fungible*. It signified a product, like a widget or a nail, that was the same, and equal to all other widgets and nails. Teachers in Boston during that era were regarded as fungible, as replacement parts. This was not a good thing: Arbitrarily breaking up faculties was not a good thing; Busing students to unchosen schools was not a good thing. But, to repeat, while the educational impact of busing was horrible, segregated schools were more so. So, the "good thing' was forced to surrender to the "necessary" one. I am glad I was not asked to find a more palatable solution: It was that complicated.

But as the expression goes, *no harm, no foul.* I was told to report to another school, not of my choosing, and as Mr. Mullin, the principal, promised, I loved it.

While the local and national news channels reported the violence, hate and chaos from several, usually very specific locations, teaching continued without incident in the majority of the different grades throughout Boston.

Like clockwork, every morning the yellow buses clogged the drive and parking area behind the Lewis Middle School and across from a hilly park that had a walkway to a municipal ice-skating rink. The students walked off the buses and down a hallway that met my homeroom before jutting off to another long hallway, then stairwells to the top two floors of classrooms. No-nonsense teachers, with miles of difficult educational journeys written on their faces, directed the kids to march quietly and orderly to assigned classrooms. When they opened their mouths, the teachers spoke with familiarity, humor, and affection. The kids responded in kind.

Afternoon departures were another story. About 10 minutes before the scheduled end of class, the top floor kids would begin their migration downstairs, in single file along the long hallways that ran parallel to me, then right angled to the door leading to the parked buses. My students had the predictable response, *If school is over for them, then it's over for us!* Teaching stopped. No matter how brilliant and grabbing my presentation was, fidgeting, and chatter caused by the distraction of the single files of top floor kids ended discussion. Fatigued, challenged, overcome, I gave in and told them to line up and get ready for the mass exit.

But I tricked them: I had to keep them busy. I told them to line up according to height, sometimes, by the alphabet, sometimes boy-girl, sometimes by the color of their coats. Anything to keep them occupied until the busing manager on the overhead speaker announced: "Mr. Muse's class to the buses!"

When the skating rink opened in early winter, I learned that most of my homeroom never skated. I went over the hill and talked to the manager who found various sizes of skates in storage. A few of the kids owned skates, and others were able to borrow some. I found a bunch back in the family home as every one of the Muses played hockey at different levels. My rink manager friend told me the place was open and unused most mornings. I worked with several other teachers in a "cluster" and with their agreement, I would march the kids out the "busing" door, over the hill, to skate for a half hour, without any administration pre-approvals, that at another time and place, would have got me fired as a teacher. It was a welcome respite for the kids from the organized chaos they were exposed to.

Most of my students were Black. The White kids generally came from the nearby Jamaica Plain Egleston Square neighborhood, which was already racially mixed, at least more so than most of Boston. So, the Boston busing experiment had less impact on the Lewis kids, until a couple of years later some teenage monsters tried to murder one of my favorite students.

I will never forget the smile Darryl Williams brought to my seventh-grade history class. He was easily the center of attention to most of the girls, and as the expression goes, he was *The Man* with the boys. He loved being a student and was happy as a friend.

In September 1979 Darryl was a sophomore at Jamaica Plain High School and had become a very talented football player. There was an away game at Charlestown High School, which like Southie, was a busing hotspot, with all of the discord, some hate, and too much violence. Three White teenagers were on a housing project roof overlooking the football field, where one of them fired a .22 caliber pistol towards the JP team. One bullet entered the neck of Darryl and left him fully paralyzed for the remainder of his life. The reaction of the city of Boston to this hate crime was similar to those events in Ferguson MO with Michael Brown, in New York with Eric Garner, George Floyd in Minneapolis, and on, and on, and on. There was a lot of protest and surprisingly no violence, as Darryl would wish.

Any one of us would have been entitled to become bitter, and indeed hateful. Darryl chose a positive path, and inspired thousands by his willingness to find and lead an extraordinary and productive life until he died in 2010. He publicly forgave his three assailants, stating: "Hate is a useless emotion that takes up too much energy."

Bobby Joe Leaster got off a Greyhound bus in Boston's Back Bay during the summer of 1969 and came into a city that required a lot of growth in race relations. That the court order, which painfully described how the city of the Sons of Liberty was so racially divided, could spawn the racist hate that surfaced during the busing era, is part of the calculus of the due process of law that Bobby Joe received. He was entitled to claim that what happened to him would not have happened to a White guy. Moreover, he was absolutely correct.

My last day of teaching, February 1977.

THE TRIAL

Several days after my trip to Norfolk, I assembled the trial transcripts and brought them to my apartment on Beaconsfield Road in Brookline. I searched my refrigerator for something to quickly eat, and called my 6 ½ year old son, C.J. who lived with his mother a few blocks away. We were in the middle of divorce proceedings, and this was a bitter- sweet ritual: I missed the little guy, and I felt a little melancholy at the end of every good night call.

I piled the transcripts next to an easy chair and opened Volume I. On the first page the clerk recited the multiple indictments charging Bobby with murder, robbery, and assault. I recalled his soft-spoken insistence of innocence and said to myself "that poor bastard" and my melancholic self-pity disappeared.

I dug into that trial record with great interest. Law students are not trained to be lawyers: That, we were told, would occur when we entered the practice. I had never reviewed a trial transcript and I was fascinated as I flipped page after page. I finally

reached the part where the rubber meets the road: The judge was on the bench and speaking to the pool of jurors assembled in the courtroom.

The judge explained the indictments to the potential jurors. As it was a charge of murder, the death penalty could be imposed. Later, he asked them individually if they had any personal views about the death penalty, and if so, would those views keep them from sitting on the case? When the trial began on June 14, 1971, Massachusetts, like most other states had a death penalty, which stayed on the books for one more year, when the U.S. Supreme Court ruled all of them unconstitutional. I imagined how Bobby felt during those moments when, one by one, potential jurors acknowledged that based on the evidence, they would be capable, and indeed willing, to order Bobby Joe to death in the electric chair.

Once selected and sworn, the jurors were bussed to 251 Talbot Avenue, Dorchester, for a view of the Talbot variety store. They circled back through the South End, past St. Botolph Street and Columbus Avenue, where the Assistant District Attorney pointed out the site of Bobby's arrest, and his apartment.

Back on the eighth floor of the Suffolk County courthouse, the clerk called the trial to order. Walter Mclaughlin, Chief Justice of the Massachusetts Superior Court, presided. Thomas Reardon, a career prosecutor, began his opening statement, as Bobby Joe sat in a defendant's box separated, and behind his attorneys, Charles Lewis and Calvin Weir.

ADA Reardon laid out the Commonwealth's case:

On September 27, 1970, at 4:00 p.m., Levi Whiteside was shot by Bobby Joe Leaster, coming to aid his wife during the robbery at their variety store. Leaster was arrested by Boston police officer Alton Frost, who was cruising District 4 in a police wagon, and who spotted Leaster at the corner of St. Botolph Street and Massachusetts Ave. and noticed that Leaster was wearing the hat, black shirt and green pants just described on the police radio.

Frost took Leaster to Boston City Hospital, where he was directed to transfer the suspect to the custody of District 3, Dorchester officers. He parked the wagon in the parking lot of the emergency room building of the hospital complex and took Leaster from the wagon to a District 3 cruiser. One officer, the driver, sat in front. The other sat next to Leaster in the rear. Frost chatted with the driver through an open window.

At the time of this transfer, Kathleen Whiteside walked through the emergency room doors accompanied by Sergeant John Downey, the District 3 supervisor who was overseeing this case. At this time Mrs. Whiteside said to Downey: *"That looks like the man who shot my husband. Can I take a closer look?"*

Downey brought her to the window of the cruiser, where she peered into it, and said "Yes, that's him," and she pointed out the birthmark beneath Leaster's eye which she remembered being on her husband's murderer. Leaster was then brought to the District 3 station for booking.

Nellie Rivera, a customer, and neighbor of the Whitesides, was in the store when the robbery occurred. She observed the two assailants as she was trying on sneakers. Bobby Joe Leaster was the one with the gun.

Nellie Rivera, Kathleen Whiteside, Sergeant Downey, and Officer Frost confirmed the facts set out in Reardon's opening by their sworn testimony.

Police Officer Andrew Murphy Jr. who was the first officer on the scene described what he observed, including the mess in the store created by the assault, the discovery of a Bulova watch lost by the shooter during the scuffle, and the location and unconscious condition of Levi before he was ambulanced to City Hospital. Dr.

George Curtis, the medical examiner testified that it was his opinion that the cause of Levi Whiteside's death, which was pronounced at 4:47 p.m. was "as a result of a gunshot wound of the chest with massive hemorrhage, homicide." Police ballistician George Gravel identified the bullet that Dr. Curtis took from Levi's chest cavity, as a .22 caliber type.

During the first day of trial, Judge Mclaughlin interrupted the witness testimony to conduct a *voir dire* of several of the witnesses, that is outside of the presence of the jury. The issue was whether the identifications of the defendant should be admitted into evidence.

The witnesses further testified that after the identification at City Hospital, Rivera and Mrs. Whiteside were brought to Station 3 in Dorchester to give statements to homicide detectives. Before they arrived, Bobby Joe had been placed in a guard room which had swinging doors. At different times, while each was ushered into a conference room, both Mrs. Whiteside, and Nellie Rivera observed Bobby Joe sitting in that guard room surrounded by up to 7 uniformed police officers.

Judge Mclaughlin considered the testimony of Alton Frost and made a finding that Frost did not know that Mr. Whiteside was already pronounced dead, before he arrested Leaster, and transported him to Boston City Hospital. Therefore, the show-up of Bobby Joe to Mrs. Whiteside in the parking lot was accidental *at a time when the police were arranging a legitimate bedside confrontation with a dying victim.*

He ruled that the confrontations at Station 3 were "infirm" and were inadmissible because they were powerfully suggestive due to all of the circumstances, and could have been avoided, by providing Leaster with an attorney, and taking affirmative steps to prevent those types of show-ups.

I got a pit in my stomach when I read the testimony of Earl Leaster, nephew, "brother" and best friend of Bobby, who was called as a prosecution witness. He testified that he had lied to homicide detective Frank Mulvee, when he stated that Bobby was with him in the South End at 3:15 p.m. the afternoon of the murder. While it concerned me that Earl's testimony was objectionable (Bobby was not claiming him as an alibi), jurors do not like deception. Earl also established that both he and Bobby had family members on Aspinwall Ave., Dorchester, several blocks from the murder scene, whom both he and Bobby had visited.

After ADA Reardon rested, attorney Lewis called Bobby to the stand.

Bobby described how he was living with his girlfriend Judy Mossoff at 527 Columbus Ave., in the South End, and that on Sunday, the day of the murder, he rose at 11:30 a.m.:

> *"I got up, and she already had cooked breakfast, and I ate, and I cooked me some pork chops later on, before I left the house, and then I were reading a book. She was helping me to read because I can't read too good. And then just before I left I was going to wash out some clothes, but around 2:30 I left, going down the street to the store to get some cigarettes."*

After purchasing the cigarettes at Bradock Drugstore, he went to visit Earl who lived around the corner. Earl was not there so he returned home. At 5:00 p.m. he returned to Earl's house, and again learned that he was not there at his apartment at 172 St. Botolph Street. He saw several friends and stopped to talk to them on the street. Just then:

> *"Two cops stopped the paddy wagon and got out, and they walked up –they walked halfway up and said, 'Hey, you' and I didn't even know they were talking to me, because my friend thought they were talking to him.*
> *He said 'Who? Me?' He said 'No, the guy in the black shirt' and I walked up to the two of them and they told me, 'We have a warrant for your arrest, murder and robbery up Talbot Avenue.' I said 'What? I just left the house at 5:00 o'clock, over my nephew house.' I said, 'Now I'm on my way back home."*

He testified that when he wa arrested he had one dollar and two house keys in his pocket, and that he was wearing a Timex watch.

During cross examination by Reardon, Bobby testified that he had been with Judy all weekend, including Saturday September 26th:

> *"Yes, I was all day because early that day we went over to the Fenway, and I played basketball, and I stayed over there all day."*

"How did you get to the Fenway" asked Reardon.

> *"We came downstairs, and we were walking up the street*

and a friend of Judith that worked with her, he passed by, and he stopped and asked her where we were going. I told him I was going over to play some basketball. He said he was going over there , too, so we got a ride over there with him."

Judy Mossoff took the stand and corroborated Bobby's testimony through the time of his arrest. She said that she was visited by two policemen approximately 2 ½ hours after Bobby last left her apartment:

"Would you tell us what happened at that time." Lewis asked her.

"Well, it was around 7:30, and they rang the bell downstairs, the bell to the downstairs door. When they came upstairs, they knocked and identified themselves as policemen and wanted to know if they could ask me a few questions. I said yes.

" I asked them to come into the house, and they asked if I knew Bobby Joe. I said yes. They asked if he lived there, and I said yes. I asked them why they were asking me these questions, and they refused to tell me.

"And when they asked me the last time I had seen him, I lied and said Friday. I said I hadn't seen him since Friday. They wouldn't give me any information except to tell me that they were looking for him for questioning. "They didn't inform me that he had been arrested. They questioned me as to his nephew, Willie Earl Leaster, if I knew him, where he lived. They asked if Bobby owned a gun. I said no because he doesn't, and I told them they could search the house if they wanted to."

She later learned from Bobby's cousin Ruby that Bobby was in Station 3 in Dorchester. She concluded her testimony by stating that at 4:00 p.m. on the day of the murder, Bobby Joe was with her at their home. "He was sitting in the house eating a pork-chop sandwich and reading from one of my books while I was helping him learn to read." ADA Reardon vigorously cross-examined Judy Mossoff and left Bobby Joe with an alibi that had exploded.

~

Three and a half hours after the jury received the case, they came back with verdicts of guilty on all three indictments. I put down the transcript shortly after midnight and spent the next half hour trying to figure it all out. From the evidence, the jury could, and indeed did, have enough evidence to convict Bobby Joe. The verdict was neither a shock nor a surprise.

I also recognized that the same jury on a different day could have found Bobby innocent of all charges. If there was nothing wrong with the trial, what on earth could I argue to the Federal Court on a claim that he was unconstitutionally restrained?

THE VERDICT

The Jury said, "First degree murder." The judge said "Jury, do you sentence Bobby Joe Leaster to death?" My knees buckled and I wanted to throw up. The jury said, "No. We don't sentence him to die." Then I heard the judge say, "Walpole. Life without parole."

I had never been arrested before in my life; I had never been to jail. I thought I was just going to fall apart when it happened to me. And that's when the faith, you know, came into my heart. I said, wait a minute, I can't just fall apart here. I said, I didn't do nothin' to be here; I didn't do a thing. But I said, I'm going to keep my faith; I'm going to keep my spirit high and somehow I'm going to beat this.... somehow, you know.

It took me about three or four years after I was locked up to realize what had really happened to me and how serious the crime was, and life without parole.

But I kept believing in the man up above; believing in God; praying. I cried many a night, asking, why did this happen to me? Why did he let this happen to me?

I kept thinking of my mother and father. All this time I had been here, and I knew how worried they were, and I didn't want them to come up here and fall apart, go off the deep end. And that's another thing that kept me going all these years. I told myself, I'm not only going to be strong for myself, I'm going to be strong for my mother and father, because they will want me to be, because they are two very religious people. My father always told us that we must leave our lives in the hands of the Good Master above us. We all went to church together, and I learned to pray every day, which I still do.

I didn't have any money, but I said, I'm going to keep filing these petitions in court, trying to get someone interested in my case and take it and work on it. And finally, in 1977 the federal court appointed the Muses to my case. They came out and talked to me, and they said, "Well, we're going to take your case. And then several months later, I seen that they was very serious about it. Right then and there I knew my prayers were getting ready to be answered after seven years. I could feel it in my heart. I could feel that the man upstairs answered my prayers by sending the Muses to me

HABEAS CORPUS

It is often called "the Great Writ."

In the year 1215 at Runnymede, England, King John surrendered some of his rights and prerogatives to nobility and other freemen when he granted the first English charter of civil and political liberties, by signing the Magna Carta.

This medieval document created the right of Habeas Corpus, which literally means "let us have the body." The writ was directed to the sheriff or other jailer based on a complaint of unlawful restraint. It is, and has been, used to bring prisoners to courts to present defenses to accusations at trials. It is the historic basis for a prompt arraignment, or "arrangement" as Mike Skerry described it, for those who were arrested. It is a cornerstone of English common law. The protection of Habeas Corpus is specifically provided in the United States Constitution.

In the case of <u>Bobby Joe Leaster vs. Michael v. Fair,</u> United States District Court, District of Massachusetts, C.A. No.77-256 M, the plaintiff was requesting the Federal Court to order the Commissioner of Corrections, Michael Fair, to release him from custody following an unconstitutional conviction in a state court.

It fell upon me to establish the unconstitutionality of Bobby Joe's incarceration. I had to prove that Bobby was denied a fair trial, which is more than simply an error free one. Whatever error I demonstrated, had to have constitutional significance.

I read and reread every important federal and state case which concerned identification evidence similar to that admitted into the Leaster trial. The law books are filled with cases that supported the proposition that whenever police bring a suspect to a witness, there was a possible denial of fifth, sixth, and fourteenth amendment rights. The granddaddy of all such cases is <u>United</u>

<u>States vs. Wade</u> , where the U.S. Supreme Court in 1967 held that:

> "It is a matter of common experience that, once a witness has picked out the accused at the lineup, he is not likely to go back on his word later on, so that in practice the issue of identity may for all practical purposes be determined there and then before the trial…The impediments to an objective observation are increased when the victim is the witness. Lineups are prevalent in rape and robbery prosecutions and present a particular hazard that a victim's understandable outrage may excite vengeful or spiteful motives."

I was stuck with the record of the case. I could not argue any facts which were not presented at the original trial. As time passed, I recognized that the cross examination of the eyewitnesses by Bobby's trial counsel was, being charitable, borderline competent. The whole point of cross is to cast doubt on the witnesses' observation. If thoroughly pursued, the jury would have understood that Mrs. Whiteside was not able to properly identify her assailant within a half hour of witnessing a doctor pronounce her husband dead from a gunshot wound inflicted several feet from her. She was grief stricken and heavily medicated. Her opportunity to observe was marginal. Her original description stated that both suspects needed shaves and were dirty looking. Bobby did not start shaving until he was in Walpole. The height description did not match. She never described the shooter as having a bruise under his eye until she saw Bobby in the cruiser and saw the birthmark under his left eye. His lawyers should have argued that the "accidental" show up at the hospital was just as suggestive and prejudicial as the one at the station which was found to be unlawful. The list went on and on. Retrial however was not an option until the appeal was successful.

~

For two years Bobby's case inched its way through countless docket entries. with guidance from Bob, and help from Tom Ford, Jim Byrne, Bobby Wheeler, and Joan Feeney, all recent law school grads. I pushed Bobby's appeal through paper filings and conferences, until September 19, 1979, when Federal Judge John McNaught heard oral arguments and took the case under advisement. The gist of my argument was that the accidental show-up to Mrs. Whiteside could have been avoided, and the failure to prevent the City Hospital confrontation was a violation of Bobby's due process right. This show-up was the root cause of the tragic misidentification which resulted in the conviction of an innocent man. I was not, as I later told the court, engaging in constitutional gamesmanship: This was a question of common sense, substantial justice, and not nit-picking lawyering.

On the night before oral argument I had dinner with Bob in the upstairs dining room of the Marliave restaurant, across from our Bromfield St. office. I had already tried a number of jury trials in Cambridge and Boston, and I did not suffer from stage fright in a court room. But this was my first time arguing a federal case, and if I was not nervous, I at least wanted to know the lay of the land.

His advice was direct:

"Make sure you make your point with McNaught. I don't care what the point is…you decide. But whatever you think is most important to the case… you make sure the judge understands it. Don't hesitate to ask him if he understands you. Answer every question he has but be sure to leave him with what you think is important."

It was not that bad. The next day, I wore my "sincerity blue" suit and sat among the sharply attired and well-spoken members of the legal guild. Decorous, oozing gentility, these were the Federal Court practitioners. It was four blocks and a universe away from the Boston Municipal Court.

Judge McNaught could not have been more gracious. He had attended Malden Catholic High School with Bob, and he immediately acknowledged that I was my father's son, and then quickly mentioned something about him being a better debater than a hockey player. All the boys in my family skated and played hockey. None of us debated. I quietly hoped that some of the debating genes were given to me, at least for the next half hour.

I first played the violins while I told the court that most of the regrettable convictions of innocent men occurred because of misidentification. I recited the litany of cases which talked about *suggestiveness, reliability, police misconduct,* and all the other buzzwords which were bullets in my memorandum. I told the court without equivocation that this identification was inherently suspect. "Look at this description which was put out on police airwaves shortly after the shooting," I stated with a buildup in the volume of my voice.

It was then that I had my first out of body experience.

I started to read the police teletype :

"Wanted for armed robbery and murder… at Talbot variety store …two unknown colored males…..

I kept speaking to the court from the script I held in my hand, as I also mentally spoke to myself, and repeated the phrase "wanted for armed robbery and murder…robbery and murder…and murder…murder." I addressed myself from outside of my body as, interchangeably, 'Christopher' and 'idiot,' as in "you idiot, if the police knew this was murder right at the scene, how could Frost be arranging a bedside confrontation with a dying victim?" I asked myself.

I stepped back into my body and *both of us* addressed the court:

> "Your honor, this teletype demonstrates that the rationale for this kind of confrontation was a pretext and a sham. Judge Mclaughlin's finding is clearly erroneous, and the out of court confrontation most assuredly must be suppressed."

Having seized the moral high ground, I sat down, knowing that Judge McNaught understood my point.

I learned then that there is a huge letdown when leaving a courthouse after an important argument. I asked all the predictable questions of myself as I departed the Federal Courthouse on Congress St. Did I get everything in? Did I confuse the Judge? Did I adequately contradict the prosecutor? Did I sound stupid?

The most important one was: Will we get a decision soon?

Chapter Four

CAMBRIDGE DISTRICT COURT

No crime story would be complete without a cameo appearance by comic actor Bill Murray.

Well not exactly, but it is a good introduction to my life the first few years after I took on Bobby's case.

I left the Malden District Court after a year and transferred five miles south to Cambridge because that court had all the jury trials and I wanted to get in front of them. Also, it was a good practice to keep on moving, meeting more lawyers, and trying different kinds of cases.

Once again, the most important one in the room was the judge. The second was the clerk. Way down on the pecking order was the defendant. Just below him was his lawyer.

The courthouse was the main one in Middlesex County, geographically the largest county in the state. A sixteen-story tower, it was built in the middle of East Cambridge, an old-style ethnic neighborhood with great restaurants and one especially good bar, The Barrister. There were only a few nights when the Barrister was not packed with the lawyers and prosecutors and court staff who pushed the cases through the courts. A lot of cases got resolved over bottles of Bud. Sometimes the terms of the deal could not be recalled the next day in court but were easily fixed with further negotiations.

Courthouses breed communities. The one in Cambridge was very welcoming and familial. I got along well with Oakie O'Connor who was clerk in the first session where all cases got called. Freddy Lindstrom became my all-time favorite court officer. Tony Coloruso a gentle giant of man was a go-to assistant chief probation officer. I deeply respected all the judges; however, my affection did not prevent quips, critiques of their rulings, or imitation of their quirks.

There is a lot of down time in busy criminal sessions. Lawyers will put their hands like barriers on their cheeks to whisper into the ears of others, usually gossip, sometimes something snide or humorous about the judge or the case being discussed. I remember one revered war horse, Al Hutton, looking over at the long bench filled with the afternoon arraignments of a half dozen men in custody. The young kids picked up for pot were scared to death. The more "court experienced" were generally smug and sometimes joking. Al pointed to an older man who looked straight ahead, said nothing, and was expressionless. "He's a lifer" Al whispered. "He has nothing but time, nothing to rush to, and he shows it."

Sometimes during a break, the older lawyers would say something helpful to the younger ones like me. I recall chatting with another war horse, Al Nugent, who had an office one floor below us on Bromfield St. I told him my first jury trial was the next day, and yes, I was a little nervous.

"Chris, when I was driving to Cambridge for my first jury trial, I threw up into my windshield just as I got into the parking lot. Kid: You're not a real lawyer unless you hurl before your first opening."

I had a caseload of the usual; juvenile, class D drugs, and simple assaults. I tried a ton of drunk driving cases. In a few years I would be charging pretty good money to defend otherwise decent people who drank too much and then drove. From time to time, I got a gun possession case. Fast forward to the late eighties through 2020 when every charge seemed to involve a firearm as the NRA-nurtured gun epidemic spread. I also had a chance to do Superior Court work. These were cases that were indicted and called for sentences in state prison. I often raised defenses of unlawful identification procedures, taking care of my clients, and honing my arguments for Bobby Joe.

This brings me to Bill Murray. In early April, a probation officer retired, and a party was scheduled at the Hong Kong restaurant near Harvard Square. The restaurant had an upstairs drinking and dancing area, which was needed as it seemed everyone who worked in the court was there to bid their fellow employee farewell. Shortly after I arrived, I heard the repeated "buzz" about a guy from Saturday Night Live dancing and hanging out. I bumped into the comedian and said, " I hear you're a funny guy." Somehow a real conversation evolved to a point that he was at my side all night at the Hong Kong. People would ask for his autograph or to do the famous WORM on the dance floor, and Bill would point to me and say, "You need to ask my lawyer."

So, what I describe as a *Stupid Night* continued across the river at my friend's Crossroads Bar, with a small entourage. When closing time arrived, I arranged for a sack full of beer from an alternative source to the liquor stores that were closed. The Stupid Night continued until 4:00 am with a heartfelt goodbye to my new best friend, who returned to the Big Apple. Its significance follows.

I predictably slept through the alarm the next morning, and I scrambled to get to the court by 10:00 am. When I arrived, the unkempt Court Officer Fred Lindstrom sat at his desk next to the side door for lawyers to enter the First Session.

The first sounds were chuckles, followed by, "Muse is in deep shit.. Muse is in deep shit." I was headed to the courtroom entrance when I was stopped by Tony Coloruso, who pressed his football tackle chest against me to impart his guidance:

"Brother Muse, you need to slow down. They've been looking for you."

"Who?"

"The judge and about ten of your clients. They called a dozen cases and Oakie kept saying "that's another Attorney Muse case."

Judge Feloney turns red every time he hears your name."

"Screw him. I'm late. So what!"

"Brother Muse, calm down. Do you know what passive aggressive is? I learned it in one of my courses. It means when you get someone arguing with you, just shut up. Agree with him and move on, say very little."

Then with a brotherly love slap to my cheek, he stepped back. "Remember, passive aggressive."

I walked through the side door as the court became instantly silent, while Judge Lawrence Feloney glared at me. I walked resolutely to the other side of the courtroom to sit at the only available counsel seat. I passed Lieutenant Ed McNally, the Cambridge police prosecutor, who could not resist, "Muse, you're fucked."

As I was directly in front of his honor, he stopped me with his words, "Attorney Muse? "

"Yes, your Honor. "

"We have called nine of your cases. Where were you?"

Everyone in the courtroom with the exception of the defendants and the judge knew exactly where I was, who I was with and why I was late.,

With Tony's words ringing in my years, I answered, "Your Honor, I wasn't here."

His beat red face turned Easter purple and he said in an unusually raised voice,

"I know you were not here; I asked where were you?"

I answered with resolve.

"I was late" and continued to my seat. Nothing else was said. Judge Feloney just shook his head, his face still as crimson as a Christmas light.

A few takeaways for a young lawyer: I think back to Malden Judge Glazer warning me to arrive on time. He was right. I fortunately was able to restore a good rapport with Judge Feloney, which was essential.

I learned about the benefit of walking away from unwinnable arguments, and I avoided a contempt of court citation that Bill Murray nearly caused.

It was while working in Cambridge that I waited for the McNaught decision. I was wound up as tight as a drum waiting for it and the distractions of Cambridge friends and fun were therapeutic. The decision came November 9, 1979, and it was a denial.

Significantly, Judge McNaught found that the reason for the show-up was to arrange a jurisdictional transfer of Bobby from one police district to another. By his silence he obliterated the crucial, unsupportable, Judge Mclaughlin finding.

But the idea that they pulled into the City Hospital parking lot to transfer Bobby from one district to another was preposterous. There was no need for it, and there was no policy in effect to do so.

If that had been the case, they would have more likely met down Mass. Ave. at the Victoria Diner. At least they could get coffee waiting for the wagon to arrive.

As disheartened as we were with his decision, we all felt we were getting closer to the truth, and that the conviction was beginning to unravel. Jim Norton was right: the cops were not going to sit around with a dead body on a Sunday afternoon.

Our belief in Bobby's innocence was not misplaced. We began the new year with greater resolve. We filed a Motion for Reconsideration, but McNaught held firm.

Our resolve remained even after our appeal to the First Circuit concluded, unsuccessfully on April 13, 1981.

LET'S BE HIS LAWYERS
FROM THE TIME OF HIS ARREST

Big Bob was undaunted; disappointed, but unstoppable.

He grasped every fact and every nuance of the McNaught ruling. The fact that the original identification process corrupted the entire trial was obvious. That the Federal Court re-characterized the circumstances surrounding the show-up was significant. However, Bob did not hesitate to discuss his view that we had an interesting, yet ultimately worthless issue for further Federal appeal. He said we needed to redirect ourselves: We had to take a fresh look at the case.

In early January, Bob became "Professor Muse" to my brother Peter and several of his classmates in their second year at Suffolk Law School. Mark Sullivan, Linda Poulos and Bobby Wheeler joined Peter one evening after class in the Bromfield Street office, with the entire case record of Commonwealth v. Bobby Joe Leaster, laid out on a conference table in front of them.

Bob told the law students:

"This will be a case study on how to try a capital case. I want you to rip the file apart. Work on the assumption that we were just retained to defend Bobby. We will investigate the case, and research the case, and prepare the case, as if we got it the day after his arrest."

They agreed and began pulling apart and abstracting the trial transcripts. Bob followed his own counsel and went out to Norfolk prison to speak to his client.

"I'd like you to take a polygraph test." he told Bobby Joe in the attorney conference room. Without discussing the operation of a lie detector, Bob simply explained, "It'll prove that you did not shoot Levi Whiteside."

"I already took one," Bobby stated to a surprised and taken aback lawyer.

"When did you do this?" Bob asked.

"The night I got arrested. The police asked me to take that test. They asked me was I right-handed: I said yes. They asked me 'could they put something on my hand.' They told me that this would tell me whether or not I fired a gun in the past 24 hours. I put both my hands in front of me, I said,

"Here test both of them.' and they did. They gave that test you want."

"Bobby, did they say they were going to give you a paraffin test?"

"Yeah, that's it, a paraffin test."

Police investigators, for decades, have had tools to detect the presence of gunpowder on a suspect's hands or clothing. There are a variety of tests that use chemical mixtures to apply to a suspect and watch for the reaction. Some are more reliable than others. They are often incorrectly bundled together under the name of the original, dated and rarely used, *Paraffin* test.

There was nothing in the case file or transcript that referenced any such test. We needed to look at the investigatory file which we learned was not available without a court order. Bob had an extra hoop to jump through to obtain it: He needed to apply to the state Attorney General for permission even though it remained a Boston police file. He did and received the necessary authorization.

Within days Bob walked through the Common to Station 4 and spoke with a Sergeant Bradbury in the identification unit, who opened up Boston police lab file No. 3160. Bob could not copy the file but was allowed to read it.

He found a report of a paraffin test performed "at 8:00 p.m. at District Three by Harold Prefontaine. B.P.D." The test was "made on the right and left hand of the defendant. A cast was made of both hands and forwarded to the F.B.I." On October 16, 1970, the F.B.I returned a report which certified that a microscopic test was made and that there was no evidence of gunpowder. The FBI labeled the result as *Inconclusive.*

If all testing conditions were met, here was proof that Bobby did not fire the gun. It was not conclusive proof, but it was some proof, in fact real good proof, and if credited by a jury, would likely become conclusive. It was not mentioned in the transcript, begging the question: Why was this evidence not used at trial?

Bob phoned Charles Lewis who came over to Bromfield St. I recall walking into the reception area and saw attorney Lewis in the same chair I sat in when Bob handed me the Leaster case. I did not see a cigar near Bob, so the conversation must have been important. Lewis insisted he never saw the gun powder residue report, and the significance of the failure of the DA to turn over evidence favorable to the defendant was not lost on him. He agreed to submit an affidavit that reported he never received it, and further:

"It is my present view, not only is such a report exculpatory, but that it so negates guilt that it would have carried the day and result in a finding of not guilty by the jury."

I was excited by the news. I had read *Brady v. Maryland* where the Supreme Court laid out the responsibility of the prosecutor in every state to turn over any evidence that tended to disprove the criminal allegations. I thought this was a home run, while Bob coolly noted it was just a base hit. But if it did not guarantee a new trial, at least it would help us get one. It was also an admission ticket to the Superior Court for further review.

And then it happened.

Months later at a hearing, Lewis did a "Dixie." He did what no lawyer should ever do: he put his minimum professional interests ahead of the interests of his client, indeed ahead of the life of his client. Lewis testified that he "now recalls getting the report" but declined to use it because the result was *inconclusive*. My heart sank as I watched attorney Lewis squirm in the witness seat in the Suffolk courtroom.

The first point, that he now remembers receiving the report can be credited to the human experience of remembering things wrong and correcting them when that memory is refreshed or refocused. The second point, that he declined using it because it was "inconclusive" was unethical on one front, and factually wrong on the other.

He signed an affidavit, under oath, after presumably a period of reflection, which stated that the report was exculpatory, and it would "have carried the day and result in a finding of not guilty by the jury." His change of opinion was unwarranted and, sadly, diminished him.

The FBI report indicated that the test result was *inconclusive* on the question of whether he had recently fired a gun, because there was no gunpowder detected. The adage, "you can't prove a negative" resounded. Detective Prefontaine testified that there were two reasons why a suspect could have fired a handgun without residue blowing back on his hands or clothing. It was possible, but highly improbable that there was no blowback. The other possibility was that the suspect had the opportunity and means to wash his hands.

This alternative was preposterous against all the known facts. The theory, that Bobby could have washed his hands after the shooting with turpentine or an abrasive soap was unrealistic. The police justified the stop and the show up in part on the fact that the murder had recently occurred. The prosecutor would have been hard pressed to argue that Bobby went home where turpentine or another cleaner was available for him to wash his hands, and then confidently walk back onto the streets. It was *reductio ad absurdum*, or simply put, absurd and fanciful. Or, as one of my non-lawyer friends declaimed, it was *Bullshit*.

The evidence that a prompt police test did *not* reveal gun powder residue was highly exculpatory. Lewis' twisted testimony led to a further claim of ineffective assistance of counsel.

Next, Bob attempted to interview all witnesses who had any knowledge of the case.

On February 4th, he wrote to Judy Mossoff Clay who had moved to New Orleans after the verdict and asked her if she knew the whereabouts of Pedro, the neighborhood barber, and Joanne, the two people Bobby was speaking to when Frost arrested him, and also Ralph Lebeau, the man who gave both of them a ride to the basketball courts on the Fenway on the Saturday before the murder.

Several weeks later Judy wrote that she had lost track of Pedro and Joanne, but that Ralph Lebeau was still in Boston. She wrote that all three had been available to testify, but that Attorney Lewis said they were not needed.

"All I can do is reaffirm Bobby's innocence. He was with me, in my house, eating a pork pie sandwich when the crime occurred on the other side of town. He didn't do it and I hope you'll be successful in your attempts to free him."

We later learned that soon after the police arrived at her apartment, they wanted to know why she was living with a *nigger*, as they rambled around her house looking for drugs, and as noted at trial, would not say why they were questioning her about Bobby's whereabouts. The reason she lied about not seeing Bobby was that the police intimidated her. And she intended to wait for Bobby's return to find out why police were interested in him.

Bob went to work looking for Ralph Lebeau. He located him working in an architect's office in Brookline. Lebeau confirmed Bobby's trial testimony, and Judy's memory of that Saturday. He signed an affidavit which recited that:

> " On September 26, 1970, at about noon, I recall it to have been a Saturday, I chanced to be driving in the Columbus Avenue-Massachusetts Avenue section of Boston and saw Bobby Joe and Judith walking along the sidewalk, I picked them up and gave them a ride to the Fenway section of Boston. I remember the foregoing very vividly because on Monday, I was informed by Judith Mossoff that Bobby Joe had been arrested for murder on Sunday."

Ralph was important because he could have rehabilitated Judy as an alibi witness. He could have negated the hasty and untruthful assertion of Judy that she had not seen Bobby all weekend. Her explanation that she lied to the police because they would not tell her why they were looking for Bobby would have become more credible.

The significance of Ralph's testimony was not lost on ADA Tom Reardon. In his final argument, he asked the jury to consider it:

> "If she had been given a ride by Mr. Lebeau, or the man that works for Model Cities with her, to the Fens, I don't know where he is. I don't know what the man looks like. It's not my job to present him. If she could account for her being with the defendant Saturday from the morning until the evening when she went to bed at 10:30 or sometime, then why Friday night? Because she had a *perfect alibi* for Saturday if she presented this barber and this man she works with. But where are they?"

Ralph Lebeau, *a perfect alibi.*

During this same time period, Bob was granted court permission to view the testimony of the eyewitnesses who appeared in front of the grand jury. Because of a change of the law, grand jury minutes were now available to all defendants. At the time of Bobby's trial, defendants had no access to them. This was because grand jury proceedings were secret, and disclosure was tightly controlled. One exception was if there was a *particularized need,* the judge would review the transcripts and if anything exculpatory appeared, it would be released to counsel. Attorney Lewis based his request on the possibility that the eyewitnesses gave inconsistent or contradictory testimony to the Grand Jury. Judge McLaughlin agreed to conduct an *in-camera* review. He apparently found nothing exculpatory: We did, though.

Had attorney Lewis received a copy of the minutes he would have been able to attack the credibility of Nellie Rivera with a prior sworn statement:

Q. What did he do, the fellow with the black hat and green pants?

A. He was behind the counter. I did not see what happened behind the counter, I was still trying on sneakers. I did not know there was a holdup. I thought it might be a friend of hers.

Crime scene photos depicted the crowded, and cluttered area behind the convenience store counter where the hurried and traumatic events occurred, visually obstructed to this corroborating eyewitness.

Nellie lived around the corner from Talbot Variety in a house she had purchased seven months before the robbery. Interestingly, she was staying eight blocks away in the other direction on the day of trial. We thought it was strange that at trial she appeared to be a reluctant witness, since she did not appear on time, and the police had to go to Dorchester and transport her to court. Several years after we took on the case, I was told that Nellie had confided to a friend that she "was very scared and that the real person got out of jail last springtime and threatened her not to say anything to anybody about the Whiteside murder."

Did she know the murderer, and was she afraid to disclose it? While we were unable to corroborate this double hearsay report, her grand jury testimony could have thoroughly eviscerated her trial testimony, and knocked out her identification of Leaster, in a case where there was no other evidence.

Lewis would also have been able to contradict officer Alton Frost's claim that he was unaware that Mr. Whiteside was dead before transporting Leaster to City Hospital.

Before the grand jury Frost testified that there was "a radio broadcast over the air of a man wanted for murder..."

Was he dead?

"I believe they just pronounced him dead. It came over the air the man was wanted for murder as well as armed robbery. That is the man we placed in the wagon."

Frost misstated crucial evidence. He had to have known that Levi was dead at the store. It is certain he went over his testimony with the ADA, saw the teletype and reviewed his grand jury testimony. That was customary witness prep. He was either incompetent or lying. It strains all credulity that it was incompetence, but neither incompetence nor deceit should excuse him. This untruth drove the train towards a conviction based on a worthless, unconstitutionally suggestive identification. The ADA did not deliver the teletype to Lewis until after Frost's testimony at the pretrial hearing on whether the hospital show up was constitutional. If attorney Lewis had the teletype before trial he could have contradicted the judge's finding of fact that the police had no idea that the victim was dead. The trial would have taken a totally different course.

Bob filed our first motion for a new trial. We all appeared in front of Judge John Irwin, a former prosecutor who ran a tightly controlled courtroom. Off the bench he was the ultimate gentleman, friendly, collegial, and courteous. On the bench, he was all business.

We had six days of hearing in June, usually for two hours each day. These were my first days doing anything substantial in the Superior Court. Years later I would be sitting where Judge Irwin presided. Now I was at a long table filed with evidence boxes and documents, sitting next to Big Bob, with Bobby Joe behind us next to a corrections officer. Coincidentally, Tom Reardon, now retired, and known to everyone in the courthouse as "Huck" sat in the adjacent jury box, and watched the proceedings, as Bob put on a succession of witnesses to substantiate and authenticate the evidence he had uncovered.

Judge Irwin denied each of the twelve claims of error that we placed in front of the court, ranging from ineffective assistance of counsel to newly discovered evidence, as well as judicial error. The decision in my mind was illogical. What I learned from it was that judges slavishly adhered to a policy of not disturbing a jury's verdict because of certain misplaced presumptions. Among them was the defendant had ample opportunity to defend his case, the judge acted without bias, the attorney was entitled to broad discretion when it came to trial strategy, and any error, if it existed, was harmless. He found that Lewis' decision not to use the FBI gunpowder residue test was a legitimate trial strategy. He found no error in the judge's refusal to release the grand jury testimony of the eyewitnesses and the arresting officer. We were looking for a new error- free trial, when at that time in Massachusetts, few were given.

We promptly filed an appeal.

One of the quirks of Massachusetts appellate procedure is that a defendant convicted of any offense except murder has the absolute right to have an appeals court review any post-conviction ruling by the trial court. Defendants convicted of first-degree murder are given an automatic review by the Supreme Judicial Court, which entails the review of the entire transcript and record of the case by at least one justice. For this reason, any subsequent appellate review must first be approved by a Single Justice, who acts as a "gate keeper" by screening meritorious appeals from the frivolous.

Justice Braucher was assigned to review the Leaster case. Because he found nothing improper in Judge Irwin's decision, he stopped further review by the entire court. We ended up on the *frivolous* side of the scoreboard.

We appealed this ruling to the full bench. In the second SJC decision in the case of <u>Commonwealth v Bobby Joe Leaster,</u> the court held that Justice Braucher had the authority to shortstop the appeal. They never addressed the gun powder test or the grand jury testimony or the failure to call Ralph Lebeau and other witnesses. The sanctity of institutional process was preserved, and the respect for the finality of convictions was shown. I am sure some judges and appellate lawyers felt great joy with this outcome. The growing legion of lawyers who assisted Bobby Joe did not.

INTROSPECTIVE

During all my years of legal work on behalf of Bobby, by every relevant measure, my life was excellent. Everyone in my large family was blessed with great health, I had a wonderful relationship with my son C.J, and my legal career was such that I was making money and having fun.

My practice grew since my first days at Malden District Court. In the fall of 1979, I joined my brother Michael as legal counsel to a local labor union, where I represented all probation officers throughout Massachusetts. In 1981, I was retained by the Boston Police Detectives Benevolent Society as its legal and labor counsel. I still pounded the hallways of the criminal courts, and also had a small civil litigation practice. I worked in interesting and sometimes controversial areas and made more money than I needed.

I came a long way from my public-school teaching days.

When I left Georgetown, I had no career direction. A Liberal Arts degree, we were told, opened up a world of opportunities. They forgot to tell us that we had to search for them.

I met an employment counselor who would assist that search. He set up an interview with a large bank. I had no interest in getting into their management training, and I guess it was obvious to the fellow interviewing me. He became as disinterested in me as I was with his bank. The counselor called me with my rejection and some advice: "Next time wear socks."

I recalled the words of a classmate who explained why he wanted to teach school after graduation. It was about giving back and having goals beyond money. I told him it was easy for him; his father was a rich real estate developer; I had student loans. But his words stuck in my mind.

I went down to 15 Beacon Street near the state house in Boston. I had an introduction to a School Department employee who helped me with a teacher application. I hit the jackpot two ways with a job offer: I was given a provisional appointment for one year to the prestigious Boston Latin School, and after I arrived at BLS, I fell in love with teaching.

I jumped into my new career with a smile on my face every day. Moonie commented that it was revenge for my fresh attitude to teachers at BC High to deal with the equally irritating city kids. I actually got a kick out of them. In any event I thought I found my calling.

But, after a few months I observed something very unsettling: Most of the teachers were dedicated and involved; but more than a few, *old timers* approaching the age of forty, were burning out. At coffee breaks I would hear things like, time to get back to the assholes, and worse. I was sure they started their careers with as much enthusiasm as I brought to my rewarding one, but something soured them. I vowed, yes *vowed*, that I would never let myself become like them, and if I found myself not wanting to go to work, I would quit.

By this time my two older brothers had become lawyers. Everyone assumed I enrolled to follow the family tradition. In fact, I decided to get a law degree so I could do something else if teaching became a dead end. If I was more mechanical, I would have likely gone to plumbing school. After seven years, I left teaching with regret. I was leaving something good to do something better, and like so much of my life, that decision was serendipitous.

I took law courses for two summers which gave me enough credits to graduate a semester early. So, as my fellow students toiled during the winter-spring of 1976, I took the Bar Exam in February, passed it in May, and got sworn in that June before I marched down the aisle with my classmates to receive my diploma, just as summer break started for the public-school teachers and kids.

My neighbor and parents' friend Judge Joe Feeney suggested that I pick up some misdemeanor appointments at his court in South Boston. I asked him, "Where do I apply?" He told me to just show up.

The South Boston District Court is on the top of a hill on East Broadway. It's a dated municipal building, and in 1976 it had a boxing gym in the basement. The main courtroom is where Matt Damon got sentenced in the movie *Good Will Hunting*. Its jurisdiction is limited to South Boston, so when folks say people in Southie settle things by themselves, they had to. Before the L Street Tavern became a tourist destination, and condo conversions exploded, Southie was a very interesting place filled with not just a lot of characters, but a place where almost everyone was a character.

One morning I went, as suggested, to the courthouse, asked the right question, and was directed to the main first floor courtroom where lawyers were appointed to cases. I sat three rows up on a far-left side and watched the proceedings. The Judge had a strong but quiet voice. The clerk in front of him did most of the talking. From time to time the probation officer said something not audible to me, but apparently understood by the judge. In a short while I observed the judge call over to his rather large court officer and whisper something at the side of the bench. The uniformed man then came over to me: "Do you mind telling me your name." I answered. He returned to the Judge for more whispering, then returned.

"The Judge wants to know if you are Bob's son." I answered in the affirmative, as the court officer went to side bar for more whispering.

He came back. "Judge Cameron wants to know what you are doing here." I told him I was hoping to get some court appointments.

Returning to side bar, there was no more responsive whispering, just a recognizable nodding by the Judge.

I continued watching the proceedings until I was startled by the even-tempered judge who raised his right hand and slammed papers on the bench and loudly exclaimed, "I can't handle this case. I put this guy in Walpole when I was a DA. Send this case to Judge Feeney. Mr. Muse, can you accept this appointment?"

"Could I? WOW! Are you shitting me? You bet I can!" I thought, as I said, most respectfully, "Yes your honor." I then accompanied the court officer with the displaced papers upstairs to the second-floor courtroom presided by the Honorable Joseph F. Feeney.

Billy H. was accused of illegally selling beer out of a window of a first-floor apartment in the "D" Street projects, after regular store hours, Sundays, and to anyone tall enough to reach the window, generally over the age of thirteen. Later I heard his nick name was *Billy-out-the -window*. I learned that Billy was part of a family involved in almost every kind of crime committed in

Southie including gambling, loan sharking and robbery. He had spent quite a few years doing major crimes, and getting repeat sentences to Walpole, just like Judge Cameron recalled. He had generally retired from that business, but like many retirees he needed to remain relevant, and earn a few extra dollars. Thus, he was given the family franchise to sell beer out the window.

This was my first time doing anything as a lawyer in a courtroom. I made extraordinary efforts to suppress the evidence and failing to establish a worthy constitutional basis to exclude the brown paper bag containing a six-pack of Narragansett beer, I listened to the recital of my first of hundreds of verdicts: *Guilty!*

At sentencing I asked the court to "continue the case without a finding." This is a procedure to defer a conviction if a first offender defendant stays out of trouble, usually for six months or a year.

"Christopher, come up here!" Judge Feeney bellowed. I stepped in front of him separated only by the clerk. "Will you look at his record. He's a career criminal. You don't continue these kinds of cases."

Then Judge Feeney began his sentencing colloquy:

"Billy H. you stand convicted of a violation of the peace and security of this community. You have been convicted of many offenses before. I should send you back to Walpole. But you had the good sense to retain this very able young attorney. Christopher Muse is one of the brightest lawyers in Boston. It is for this reason, and this reason alone, I order that you pay a fine of $200."

Before the judge could say another word, Billy-out-the-window whipped out a bankroll and put two "C" notes in front of the clerk and walked out very relieved.

That afternoon I regrouped at my father's office and received two phone calls originating in Southie. The first was from Billy H.

"Hey counsellor. It sounds like you're the guy to see in Southie. A kid down the street in the projects was arrested for rape. Can you take his case?"

"Of course," I said. "Give me his phone number."

The second call was from Judge Lawrence Cameron:

"Chris, John Roche, my law court clerk who provides me with legal research is taking time off for the Bar Exam this summer. I have funds to hire a replacement. My question is, would you be interested in the position, just for the summer."

My answer then was the same earlier when he asked if I would accept appointment to Billy H.'s case:

"Could I? WOW ! Are you shitting me? You bet I can!" I thought, before I appreciatively said, "I would love to."

That summer I spent every morning in a trial session, and watched lawyers ply their trade for defendants and cases of every variety. There were many drunk drivings, minor assaults, some drug possessions, and disturbances of the peace. The serious cases, felonies, were heard by the judge in Probable Cause hearings. There were three rape cases, two murder cases, one where a body was thrown in a dumpster, and more than a few armed robberies.

I learned a lot. First, I saw how cases were presented. Second, I saw how judges dispensed justice, usually very fairly. Third, I saw how probation officers like Billy Hanrahan, and Bill Gillespie, helped defendants reconstruct their lives. Lastly, and most importantly, I decided that "I can do this too !"

I teach a Trial Practice course at Boston College Law School. I promise my students at the first class that at the end of the semester, they will be able, if they wish, to become trial lawyers. They will each be able to say, "I can do this too."

So, when I ended the summer, as Judge Cameron offered to recommend me for a position with either the District Attorney or the Mayor's Corporation Counsel, I thought long and hard about leaving teaching, and doing something I knew I wanted, and could do. I was hesitant, and returned to the Lewis School, but with the urge to become a trial lawyer growing. Six months later, I made that break, driven by an unexpected opportunity and an enthusiastic love of the law.

Now, a few years later, with all the great things going on in my life, there was one cloud on my horizon. I do not want to magnify its size or darkness, but the repeated rejections by the courts of each of Bobby's appeals were painful. It was not just the thousands of hours of work and energy that Bob, I, and other lawyers contributed to what was an ongoing losing cause, that affected me. Part of it was my disappointment with the courts, almost as if they betrayed my trust in them. What was most burdensome was the strength of my conviction that Bobby was innocent, and no matter what we collectively did, we ultimately did nothing; He was still in jail and would be for the rest of his life and mine.

We had become much more than lawyer and client. Bobby was the first to call my mother on Mother's Day, Christmas, and Thanksgiving. I had to tell him that being the first to call her made all the Muse boys look bad. He laughed me off but continued as he had always done. I received so many phone calls from him in the early mornings, that I installed a phone in my bathroom, because he, almost without fail, rang me while I was in the shower. Bobby watched my son grow from the times he accompanied me on jail visits, and, as Bobby's time in prison progressed, during monthly furloughs.

Throughout it all Bobby remained an incredible model of hope, and as such, inspiration to his lawyers. When notice of each lost appeal reached our office, it would set off a period of gloom and bitterness at a system that either did not work or did not care.

On March 23,1982, Bob wrote to box 43, MCI Norfolk, Norfolk Mass:

Dear Bobby Joe:

The decision came down regrettable but expectedly. We are going to file another motion for a new trial based on statements of Mrs. Whiteside. I will be down to see you in ten days.

Keep up your courage pal.

I knew that Bob's continued show of strength imbued Bobby with hope and continued confidence in our representation. Bobby had deep faith, which lent itself to optimism. But I think it was the unswerving commitment of Big Bob that sustained Bobby Joe's hope and supported his faith in leaving his life in the hands of the Good Master above us.

Those who came to know my father understood that nothing would ever stand in his way to do the right thing. This was how his friends from Malden Catholic and BC saw him. And since I got to meet many of his Marine Corps brothers, I knew this was how they also remembered him.

We kept a powder blue book at our Green St. home titled *The World War II History of Marine Corps Aviation.* I often opened up this large volume to a paragraph which described how Lieutenant Robert F. Muse flew into the crossfire of the SS Wiley, a Destroyer, spraying an incoming Japanese suicide bomber. Bob shot down the Kamikaze pilot, saving the ship. For this he was awarded the Distinguished Flying Cross. It was a small piece of WWII history that sparked pride in me and my siblings.

In the late eighties Bob received a letter from the captain of the SS Wiley who was organizing a reunion of all the shipmates and was determined to "find the guy that saved our asses." He was referring to May 4, 1945, when the Wiley was on a rescue mission headed towards another Destroyer, the SS Luce which had been sunk from an earlier enemy attack. On course to the *Luce,* the *Wiley* came under attack by six Japanese aircraft.

Harvey Jacob who was on Wiley's bridge recalled how the sailors shot down five Japanese planes, but one avoided radar detection and was zeroing in the *Wiley*. Then he saw the Corsair that Bob was piloting come out of nowhere:

"He puts his stick down and went into a dive. All of a sudden, he comes flying across, right through our fire and is shooting at this plane until he "splashed" it, sparing the 330 men on the Wiley as well as the survivors on the Luce, and then flying into the horizon."

That pilot went nameless until the *Wiley* Captain saw that paragraph in the Aviation History, located Bob and invited him to the reunion. He became an honorary member of the *Wiley*. An interesting sequel was a letter from my high school friend, Jodie Graul, who after publication of the "Reunion'" story in the *Boston Globe*, wrote my father: "Dear Mr. Muse. My father was on the *SS Luce.* Thank you."

Bob never spoke of that incident in a bragging way. He described the defeated pilot as an honorable serviceman who sacrificed his life in defense of his country. Bob once commented that he was "as much a Kamikaze pilot flying for the Marine Corps as any Japanese flying for their air force. " In his later years, after he confronted the absolute insanity of war, he prayed every day for that unknown airman. Without a hint of the maudlin, he explained that "it came from the C Christian feeling of charity, the love for your brother."

His was a big heart. I went through my adult life hearing from many who received acts of kindness; small favors, guidance, comfort, money, getting someone out of a jam, free legal representation, friendship when others had doors slammed shut on them, and his famous hugs. If Big Bob could show charity towards the pilot that was shooting to kill him, and courage when it was happening in the flak filled Pacific sky, boundless charity to this unfairly imprisoned young man who came to be treated like a son came easily.

And so, it was no surprise that once we finished our brooding, we gathered in the Bromfield Street office to restart our battle to get Bobby Joe his justice.

BAY STATE CORRECTION CENTER, 1979

Like Bobby, most inmates began their prison journey in Walpole. At the time, it was the most dangerous prison in Massachusetts. It had a classification unit that would assess each arrival for suitability for each level of incarceration from minimum to maximum. A long-term assignment could be hellish. Prisoners really do make license plates. It is also the best work assignment in Walpole because it meant eight hours outside of the row above row of steel barred cages. Rehabilitation got only lip service, as the main purpose was to isolate and punish. Prisoner violence was and is epidemic. Bobby's work partner Albert DeSalvo, *the Boston Strangler,* was murdered in his cell. Years later, when author Sebastian Junger was researching a possible, indeed probable, wrongful conviction that evolved into *A Death in Belmont,* I connected him with Bobby. Sebastian made a compelling, but purposefully not a definitive, case that Albert Desalvo strangled a woman in Belmont, his hometown, when he was but one year old, and the man accused of strangling more than a dozen women in greater Boston, was working with a contractor remodeling his parents' home at the time of the murder. Roy Smith, a Black man who had been cleaning the victim's house was convicted. Sebastian wished to speak with those who served time with DeSalvo. I recall Bobby's response was that he was scared to death of him and deliberately stayed far away from him.

When Bobby was classified as eligible for Norfolk, he was headed to a prison built in 1930 under the supervision of a corrections visionary, Howard Gill whose policy statement was futuristic and humane:

"Norfolk seeks not only to guard securely the men committed to its safekeeping, but as a fundamental policy to assume its responsibility for returning them to society…as better men capable of leading useful, law-abiding lives."

Many of Gill's progressive ideals were met. Dormitory style rooms, athletic facilities, and educational opportunities continued through, Bobby's stretch at Norfolk. It was however, as Bobby's shanking and hospitalization demonstrates, a bad place with many bad convicts.

Bobby Joe's transfer to the Bay State Corrections Center was a gift from God. This minimum-security facility was built at the east corner of the Norfolk Prison walls. There are no gates or walls surrounding it. But, as the corrections officers and the inmates often comment, one substantial transgression, and it's back behind the walls. It housed many who had served substantial time for offenses including murder. One officer told me those convicts were the easiest to manage, the most capable of rehabilitation, and least likely to recidivate.

The dormitory style two-man rooms, dining and recreation facilities permitted free movement throughout the building and the outside recreation area. Picnic tables were scattered around a running track for family visits.

I got transferred to Bay State Corrections in 1979. This is a big minimum-security building outside the wall of Norfolk. You have to be trusted to get there. I had a good record. There are no walls. When I arrived, I felt like I was released. It took me a little time to get used to living outside the wall.

Some nice people were there. Joannie Lyons was my case worker. There was Omar Raheem, they called him Reef, Ron Harris, Carl Griffin, Warren Gibson who they called "Cocheese," who is dead now, Willie Smith 1, and Willie Smith 2, that's how they called out for them on visitors' day. Chris Scott was my best friend. I didn't have many visitors. Chris' sister Toma came up from Brockton, and his other sister came up from Virginia, and also his mother. Whenever they came, they always included me in their visits like I was part of the family. They treat me like family.

They had a furlough program. I got let out for 24 hours and I got a ride both ways with Earl. You had to return on time. If you were really late, or just didn't show up you would lose privileges. I was given 113 furloughs from Bay State. It was freedom. We were treated like human beings. But we always knew we had a jail cell waiting for us. When we returned, we were strip searched. We stood naked waiting sometime a long time for the officer to search us. That's when we really knew we were just prisoners.

But we were treated like human beings. The superinten-dent, the corrections officers, they talked to us like human beings. It was a very good place for a prisoner, but it was prison. I remem-ber all the times you and Mr. Muse would visit me, and when it was time I walked you to the front door and I watched you walk to your car, and I thought, that was freedom. That must be wonderful to get in your car and drive away. I knew one day I would. But when I watched you in the parking lot, I admit it, I was sometimes sad.

I represented Luis Tiant, the Red Sox pitching icon, after he finished his professional baseball career. There was no more popular a figure in Boston during the '75 World Series than the Manchu mustached right hander, son of Havana. Anyone with a television was glued to the games when maybe, just maybe, the Curse of the Bambino could be vanquished. That included the in-mates in the Massachusetts prisons. Everyone, whether with the privilege of a Fenway seat or a crowded place in front of a TV, lived the magic of those seven games. Even with their loss of the world championship, when the Red Sox returned to being "bums," Looie remained a hero.

One night over dinner Luis told me how much he enjoyed visiting the sick in hospitals. "It was good for the patient, but really good for me. " He enjoyed doing it without publicity, and espe-cially when the patients were children. I knew Bobby Joe was feel-ing low about the endless unsuccessful appeals, so, "How about prisoners" I asked, "Can you visit Bobby Joe?" In typical fashion, without a bit of hesitation, he agreed.

I drove Luis to the Bay State facility. There were no walls, and the entrance did not have metal detectors and endless doors to pass through. It could have been a college campus residence. I sur-prised the officer handling the visitor check in. My name was writ-ten many times: this was the first for El Tiante. The director of the facility thought it would be great if every inmate met him. Instead of bringing them all down to the common room, he suggested we walk through the dormitory. So, with Bobby Joe at our side, we went up to two long corridors of rooms and Bobby introduced his friends to the most beloved Red Sox player of the time.

A good percentage of the inmates were lifers, doing time for murder. Each knew that any violation of the rules would send them back behind the wall. At that time there was a flexible, albeit difficult path to commutation of the life sentence and then parole. This incentivized the prisoners to improve themselves with training, education, substance abuse counseling and treatment, and few disciplinary reports. They also had the opportunity to go home for twenty-four hours each month through the coveted furlough program. This incredibly successful rehabilitation tool was quickly eliminated when the infamous Willie Horton escape publicly exploded during the George Bush - Michael Dukakis 1988 presidential campaign.

Horton was a first-degree lifer in Massachusetts who failed to return from furlough. Instead, he traveled to Maryland where he violently raped a woman, pistol whipped her fiancé, then robbed both. It was a pivotal point in the campaign, causing many to view the portrayal of a dangerous Black man as racist. It cost an election and caused Massachusetts to retrench its prison rehabilitation efforts.

As we walked the halls and Luis took time to speak to each inmate, sign an autograph and encourage him to take care of himself, I was struck by the humanity of each: Luis giving, the inmate sharing. With Bobby, knowing his story, Luis told him, "Stay strong, boy, you did nothing, you don't belong here, but you have to be strong." Then he turned to Bobby's roommate Chris and said, "You belong here, but you got to be strong, it's hard, but stay strong."

Everyone was excited to meet Looie. They all said, "Man how does your lawyer know a superstar. How did he get him to come see us? Wow, Luis Tiant came personally to see us. They were just excited. It was a very nice day at Bay State.

Chapter Five

THE APPEAL- PART TWO:
WE HAVE TO FIND THE REAL MURDERERS.

I first met Bo Burlingham in the Bromfield St. office. The *Phoenix* was Boston's premier alternative newspaper that had a reputation for beating out the big press papers with front page stories of corruption and scandal, written by reporters, mostly young, who doggedly pursued them. Bo was my age, and a freelance writer from Cambridge who heard about Bobby Joe's case from one of my father's former clients. Bo started his journalism career with the *Phoenix*, later becoming Editor of Inc. Magazine, and then author of several books. He listened to Bob for a few hours, and excited by the case, he convinced the *Boston Globe* to commission him to write a magazine piece about it. After meeting Bobby, he became convinced of his innocence. He was a convert who later became a zealot, which we shall see, was a good news, bad news story.

Bo first went to see Kathleen Whiteside. He has that special gift that invites people to open up to him. So, in a short while, Kathleen recounted that horrible day in her life, the robbery and its immediate aftermath. She described how the police arrived at the store and EMT's put a sheet over the face of her husband before placing him in an ambulance.

"I told them to carry him to a hospital. They said that he was dead. I said 'No, he is not. Just get him to the hospital. They were going to go to Carney. Then a call came and said they brought him to City, so they brought me to City "

The Carney is a full-service hospital in Dorchester a little more than a mile from the variety store.

At City Hospital Mrs. Whiteside noticed Bobby Joe in a police wagon:

"I said 'That is the guy who killed my husband.' the policeman said 'Don't say nothing. We want you to take a closer look.' They carried me out of the cruiser. They made him get out and walk around and I said, 'That is him.'"

The significance of Kathleen's statement was not lost on Bo; it proved that the hospital ID was a set up. It was not for a dying victim, and it was not an accident. Bo shared the information with us.

I was excited by this development. It confirmed my first instinct: they didn't bring Whiteside to City for medical care: they were bringing him to the Medical Examiner's office at the morgue. Surprisingly, Bob was skeptical: "We can't even get the Supreme Judicial Court to look at this case," Bob stated with muted anger. "We'll keep knocking on their door, but Bobby is not going to get a new trial until we tell the court who really did it. That's the reality."

Ron Kovner, who had been working side by side with Bob for the past several years agreed. "They'll keep looking and finding a way to knock us down," he stated.

"Well, that's it," I thought, "now we have to find the killers."

Bob then recounted how he learned about the paraffin test. "Bobby didn't tell me about that until I asked him about the polygraph test, which we have not yet done. He has to know more about this case than he's told us." I chimed in:

"He's told me that people in jail have told him they know who killed Whiteside. I ask him 'Who told you this, Bobby' he says he forgets, and I say, They know who did it, and you forget. Don't you think that might be important?"

My father added:

"Bobby knows more than he's told us. I want to put him under hypnosis. I want to bring him back to his arrest and make him tell us everything he saw and did that weekend. A good hypnotist can make him remember if he farted."

This was an extraordinary tactic. I had never heard of hypnotized testimony coming into evidence. But this would be an investigative tool. I had heard that it had been used to get victims to recall some details of a traumatic, sometimes criminal, event, but I could not recall any specific details. It was a chancy undertaking. But, hey, why not ?

Polygraph test results were then admissible in criminal trials, with certain requirements and limitations. Bob hit the reset button to do what was detoured by the disclosure of the paraffin test. "Let's hook him up with Joe Murphy and put him on the machine," Bob directed.

A few weeks later Joe Murphy, who had spent dozens of

years operating lie detection equipment, journeyed to Norfolk Prison. He tied rubber bands around Bobby's arms as though he was taking his blood pressure, which, in fact he was. Following a procedure known as "the positive control technique" Joe asked four predetermined questions and analyzed Bobby's responses:

Q. When Mr. Whiteside was shot, were you standing right there?

Q. When that gun was fired, were you holding the gun?

Q. Do you know for sure who shot Mr. Whiteside?

Q. Did you shoot Mr. Whiteside?

> In his report, Joe wrote: "It is the opinion of this examiner that they (the graphs) support the truthfulness of your client, Bobby Joe Leaster, when he denies responsibility for or criminal involvement in the crime for which he is convicted."

When I reviewed his opinion letter, Joe Murphy told me that on three of the questions Bobby's truthfulness rang clear as a bell. There was no doubt that Bobby gave absolutely truthful responses to those questions asking if he shot or participated in the shooting of Levi side. However, Joe was troubled by Bobby's response to the third question; "Do you know for sure who shot Mr. Whiteside?"

> "His answer was kind of ambiguous. He's not lying when he says his answer. It's just that his response to that question does not register as strong as the others. He's not lying… it's just strange…"

A few Saturdays later Bob, Ron and I went to Bay State. It was a now familiar routine, and the corrections officers could not be more accommodating. Robert McGrath, a forensic hypnotist from Connecticut, was retained to place Bobby into a hypnotic trance and question him. My mother also attended. She had assisted during the previous hearings, and would continue until the fall, when she was appointed a judge in the Suffolk County Probate Court.

At 10:30 a.m. Mr. McGrath put on a magic show that lasted until 1:00p.m. After setting up the room with the video equipment, Mr. McGrath placed Bobby in a chair and for approximately ten minutes directed him to relax, to slow down his breathing, to loosen his muscles, and then he took him down a 12-step stairway of time, each step being a year, until on the twelfth step he was back to the morning of Friday September 25, 1970.

For the next 2 ½ hours Bobby sat virtually motionless, with only the fluttering of his closed eyelids and his mouth moving. It was astounding.

McGrath slowly took Bobby through each routine event of Friday…playing basketball with his friend Jack Clay, showering, waiting for the arrival of Judy. When Bobby spoke of the cheeseburgers he had for lunch, his eyelids almost smiled, and from his voice you could sense how much Bobby enjoyed that meal.

Bobby gave a chronology of everything that happened on Saturday, and that fateful Sunday. By his voice he appeared terror stricken when he was placed in a wagon after being accused of murder. He recounted with specificity each and every conversation with the police, and each of the identifications by the witnesses.

During the session we were allowed without speaking to hand Mr. McGrath notes which contained questions we wanted answered.

I gave McGrath a piece from my legal pad:

"Ask him: 'Did anyone ever tell him they knew who did the murder?'" I wrote.

McGrath posed the question.

Yes.

"Do you know who those people are?"

Paul McKenzie.

"And who else?"

Frank Grimmons

He gave a physical description of Frank Grimmons. And stated that Grimmons was the one who personally knew the killers but would not identify them. The conversations took place in the 70's, '73, '74 or '75 in either the Norfolk prison laundry or the yard.

When Bobby was taken out of his trance, we told him of the hypnotic disclosure.

That's Frank Brimage, not Grimmons. That's right he told me; he knew who did it. That's right, Bobby now remembered. He told us that McKenzie was a friend in prison who was also known as 'Slaughter.'

I was able to track down Paul McKenzie who had just been released from Charles Street jail, and I obtained his current address. I learned that Brimage was doing time in Concord

Reformatory for a bank robbery. I was extremely cautious. I felt there was no way a lawyer or a private investigator could get close to either of them. "There must be another way" I thought; And there was.

I called Dan Mahoney, the Detective's Union president, and asked him to help me. It's a funny thing about cops; they generally respect aggressive lawyers. They get irritated by them, but they usually respect them. Dan made an appointment for me to see Deputy Superintendent Jack Barry, who oversaw the Boston Homicide Unit. At his office, I told Deputy Barry that there may have been some problems with police procedure, I did not want to embarrass any officers, but they made a mistake, and Bobby Joe was innocent.

"These things can happen. Let me see what I can do," he responded kindly.

In the next several days he assigned Detective Tom Cashman to interview both Brimage and McKenzie. 'Slaughter' told Tom that there were those conversations, but that he did not know who was involved, or who made any admissions.

Frank Brimage was our best hope, and Detective Cashman wrote him a letter addressed to the Concord Reformatory. He described the Whiteside robbery/murder and asked him if he had any information about it. The letter was short and sweet, and for a long time we heard the phone *not ringing,* as Brimage did not respond.

This was a large bump in the road but not a dead end. We went ahead and filed a motion for a new trial based on the Kathleen Whiteside statement, the grand jury testimony of both Nellie Rivera and Alton Frost, and the polygraph test results. We presented the transcript of the hypnotic interview to corroborate Bobby's claims concerning his arrest and identifications. We submitted this together with the previously argued evidence. The motion with exhibits was voluminous, and drafting it took dozens of hours. It was filed on July 2, 1982, with an attorney's affidavit which authenticated each piece of information and document in the pleading. I recall we were relieved to finish it before the long holiday weekend.

We had no word from the court through Labor Day. That was a good sign, as we figured the judge needed time to write a thorough and *good* decision. A few weeks later we received in the mail the order that the motion was denied by Judge Irwin, without a hearing, based on the absence of an affidavit signed *by the defendant* which raised any substantial post-conviction issues.

Our post-decision meetings at Bromfield Street began to resemble support group therapy sessions.

We tried to make sense of Judge Irwin's order. Our claims for post-conviction relief were set out in intelligible form; Sixteen separate exhibits were attached to it. All the new evidence claims concerned information known either to the attorneys or the witnesses who provided affidavits. We did not submit an affidavit from Bobby Joe because, quite simply, he had nothing to personally add to the motion.

We decided that Judge Irwin's reliance on the absence of an affidavit signed by Bobby was hyper-technical, and that we had satisfied the rules of pleading. We had grounds for an appeal and would file one.

I urged Bob and Ron to slow down and go through the order of dismissal more cautiously: I had a plan.

"Rule 30 does not require an affidavit" I stated, while reading the relevant provision from the Massachusetts Rules of Criminal Procedure. "Irwin did not find that we failed to raise a substantial issue: The only reason he gave was that Bobby Joe, himself, did not file an affidavit" I said as I repeated the one sentence order from the court papers. "We say we don't need an affidavit: Irwin says we do. Why get into a pissing contest? If he wants an affidavit from Bobby, let's give him one." I proposed that we file a Motion for Reconsideration, and have Bobby sign an affidavit. We all agreed.

Within a week I drove out to Bay State Corrections and sat down with Bobby for several hours, after asking, "In your own words, tell me why you did not get a fair trial." We both went through all of the developments since his conviction, and with my prompting he acknowledged that his trial would have been fairer if certain evidence was presented. We talked about the paraffin test, the Ralph Lebeau statement, the exculpatory grand jury statements of Nellie Rivera, the deliberate, as opposed to "accidental" show-up, and the polygraph evidence.

I took my notes back to my home and pulled an all-nighter as I drafted an affidavit. I started around 8:00 PM and with trial transcripts and dozens of pages of post-conviction papers strewed on my kitchen table, I organized all the important facts that supported Bobby's claim for a new trial. I remember shuffling a Bruce Springsteen album, and drinking too much coffee, as I worked through early morning to the sound of "The Boss." I would not go to bed until it was finished. I began to nap after first light.

On October 4th I returned to Bay State Corrections in the evening to obtain Bobby's signature. It was my son's birthday, and his friend Brendan Wynn had come by for a small party. I took the two twelve-year-olds to the prison. On the way each of them reenacted one scene or another from the classic movie *Stir Crazy*: "That's right, I'm bad. I'm bad," either C.J.. or Brendan repeated during the 45-minute trip. When we arrived at the minimum-security setting, and the boys met and observed convicts, usually muscle bound, and guards, their attitudes changed to seriousness and timidity.

Bobby reviewed the affidavit and signed it. I endorsed it as a notary and returned home.

The boys had been given a copy of the three-page affidavit, and a thumbnail sketch from me of the history of the case.

"How could he have done it if he was wearing a Timex watch when he was arrested, if the guy that did the murder lost a Bulova watch at the store?" C.J. asked. "If he's gonna go home to put on a new watch, why didn't he change his clothes too." he added.

"Good point" I said.

"This sucks." said Brendan.

"Two more converts." I thought.

UNTIL JUSTICE IS DONE

We filed the Motion for Reconsideration with the required defendant affidavit. It was procedurally intact, and we were notified that we would have a hearing in late December to overturn the first decision. I had worked feverishly to research and draft a memorandum of law that I hoped would convince the judge to give us an evidentiary hearing to argue for a new trial. Because it was my memo, I would orally argue the motion.

We travelled up to the Suffolk County Courthouse, a place that always had a welcome mat out for Bob, and where I spent hours every month trying cases and doing my union business with the court officers, probation officers, and Boston Detectives who worked in the building.

Bob and I took seats at the defendant's counsel table, Bob to my left, and I close to an aisle which separated us from the prosecutor's table, where ADA John Kiernan sat. I spread the motion, affidavit, exhibits and memo in front of me. The Judge entered the chamber, the clerk announced the case, and I stood up to address the court.

I was two minutes into describing the background of the case, when Judge Irwin started firing questions at me. "Didn't you already raise this? Didn't I already rule on that?" he asked.

"I would like to know some case which stands for the proposition that polygraphs are admissible on motions for new trial, or motions for post-conviction relief." he demanded.

I had no case to cite, so I winged it.

"Your honor, as you are well aware, there is the great, wonderful body of law which ultimately governs motions for new trials and that it is for a trial court judge to review whether substantial justice has been done."

"There is also the great body of law that somewhere along the line there should be finality to criminal cases." the judge retorted.

Before I could further respond, Bob pushed himself halfway out of his chair and stated: "not until justice is done."

I sensed the beginning of a dog fight. I began talking about polygraph evidence, but after a few seconds Judge Irwin took me to the woodshed over my opinions concerning its evidentiary value. After four or five protracted minutes he concluded:

"So, I don't want to sound contentious, but I am not persuaded at all by any talk about polygraph tests."

Strike one.

Judge Irwin recalled how he had conducted exhaustive hearings on the first motion for a new trial.

"As soon as that is denied and you go through this appellate process again in which you don't have any success, then it is right back here again with some other allegations. How long do you think the courts have to put up with that type of approach?" he demanded.

Bob was getting agitated. *Tell him until justice is done.* he muttered in the loud and muffled tone known as an Irish whisper.

I told the judge that some divorce cases took more time and got more attention resolving property disputes. I quickly realized that this was the wrong tack. As the court transcript recorded:

The court: I am inquiring of you as to how long you think that under the rules of this court and the decided cases we have to continue to hear so-called motions for post-conviction relief which are literally flooding the courts of the Commonwealth right now and concerning which nobody seems to have any concern about the dissipation of the resources of this court. That's what I want to know.

In *sotto voce,* Bob to my left interpreted this inquiry and told me:

"Until justice is done. Tell him until goddam justice is done."

I was in a tough spot: I had the choice of being a fresh prick to the court, or a cowardly son to my father. I knew what I had to do.

Mr. Muse: The short answer is *until justice is done.*

I waited for the explosion. It came.

The court: Justice as you describe it, right? Your description of justice is your concern. My description of justice has to be beyond your limited concern for the representation that you have attached to you as of the moment. The perspective is a little larger than that, Mr. Muse, from the perspective of this particular bench, and it involves the resources of a lot of people. It involves, really, considerations that go far beyond the limited perspective that you have as counsel for one particular defendant.

Then to this drama came a proverbial pregnant pause: It was actually and uncomfortably a full nine-month gestational pause.

Finally, the judge spoke. He directed us to submit an affidavit which would list the witnesses we intended to call, and the issues we would address. It was delivered the next day.

We left the courthouse with mixed feelings. On the one hand, Judge Irwin was not bashful about his view of our case: On the other, he asked us to submit a list of witnesses.

I actually liked Judge Irwin in spite of his position on the case. I knew he sometimes liked to vent from the bench and then would do the opposite when he left it. I used to tell people that I grew up with almost a dozen siblings. I did not mind getting yelled at. I was used to it.

We were assigned a hearing date for the following June.

FRANKLY SPEAKING

It was early April when I was in the Bromfield Street office when Bobby called me collect. By this time Bobby had become a "trusty" such that he enjoyed not only overnight furloughs but also jobs away from prison. He had been recently assigned to a construction detail which did painting and remodeling work in state owned buildings throughout Greater Boston. Our conversations hit upon every possible topic from the Celtics to my son, until as always, we talked about his case.

I had nothing further to report. We were preparing for the motion hearing. We felt comfortable with all our positions. I told him this last week, and the week before that, and the week before that as well. We had a big hole in our case and out of the blue I said:

"I wish I could get in touch with Frank Brimage."

I just saw him, Bobby replied.

"Huh?"

He's at Bridgewater.

Bobby explained that he was doing construction work at the prison complex in Bridgewater, a southeastern Massachusetts town, and had seen Brimage who was serving time there.

I said hi, and we talked.

"You're shitting me. Tell me that again."

Bobby repeated it and told me he was returning to Bridgewater the next day.

"Will you be seeing him again?" I asked, "And, can you get him to talk to us?"

Bobby said that he could see Frank again and he would call me back.

I ran into Big Bob's office and saw a big smile on his face as I told him about this obviously important development.

The next day Bobby called and told me that Brimage would talk only to his lawyer. We pressed Bobby to get Frank to let us bring a third person. You always need a witness to a support a person's statement. Brimage was street smart to that as well, and his answer was not unexpectedly, *no*: he would meet with just one lawyer. Bob, alone, would travel to Bridgewater and speak with Brimage.

When he met Frank Brimage in the attorney's visitor room at MCI Bridgewater on May 9th, Bob knew there would be obstacles. He knew how to show respect and create a bond with any one with whom he might speak, and he did that with Frank. We knew that Bobby Joe described Big Bob as a second father and as a man that Frank could trust. After a while Frank opened up to Bobby Joe Leaster's lawyer and dad.

Bob had four meetings over a few weeks. Patiently, Bob described the work we had been doing for Bobby Joe, that we knew he was innocent, and that he would remain in prison until the real killers were identified.

Brimage was cautious. He stated that he knew who murdered Levi Whiteside but would not disclose his identity. He agreed that Bobby Joe was his friend, and that he would like to help him, but he was not going to implicate anyone, and end up doing "p.c." –protective custody- time. At that moment Bobby Joe was passing by an outside window, and with a big smile, waved to his two friends inside. Frank noticeably softened as a smile stubbornly crept onto his "I'm a hardcore con" face.

Bob pressed on.

"Then tell me something about him without naming him. Give me some clues. You don't have to identify him by name."

That worked.

The "suspect' grew up on Intervale Street: he was 17 or 18 when the murder occurred; he was Jamaican; he had escaped from a pre-release center, either Bay State pre-release, or Harrison Avenue pre-release center, during the spring of 1982, and was doing rap up time in Concord prison.

When Bob returned to the office, he had difficulty keeping a cigar in his mouth with a smile that interfered with clutching it as he spoke. "We just need to find a Jamaican in one of two pre-release centers who got bounced in the spring of 1982," he told me.

I went to work with the information by giving it to an investigator with good contacts in the prison system Three days later I was told that only one person in the system fit the criterion: Kelsey Reid.

Bob returned to Bridgewater the following day and continued his dance with Frank. No, he would not give him any initials. Slaughter McKenzie knew more than him, he stated. Slaughter went to school with the suspect. It was in Concord that Brimage overheard the conversation where the suspect talked about the murder, "and another person was picked up for it wearing a hat just like I had on." When asked if he knew if Slaughter had recently seen the suspect, Brimage inadvertently slipped: "I don't know where Kelsey lives."

Bob saw Bobby Joe doing a work detail. After he finished with Frank Brimage, he spoke with Bobby.

"If I suggested the name 'Kelsey,' would that mean anything?"

Kelsey Reid, Bobby instantly responded.

"Who told you that name?" Bob asked.

"He (Brimage) didn't tell me. Slaughter told me."

During the next two weeks we learned everything we could about Kelsey Reid. He was a junkie who robbed small stores: convenience, liquor, and the like. We learned that he ran with Peter Gardner, another junkie from the same neighborhood. In fact, Kelsey and Peter were arrested and convicted of robbing a liquor store on October 14, 1970, just 17 days after the Talbot Variety hold-up and murder. What was most interesting was the District 4 police report which described how an officer chasing Reid observed him throw an object into a vacant lot. "Further search turned up a fully loaded .22 caliber Harrington and Richards revolver, serial number ad 16504." It was just like the one that was used to kill Levi Whiteside.

Bob returned to Bridgewater as pleased as the cat that swallowed a canary. He asked Frank about the letter Detective Tom Cashman sent him. Frank told Bob that he received it and confronted Kelsey Reid about it:

"I walked right over to Kelsey and I said to him, 'They're still looking for you for the Talbot Ave. murder'

He asked me,' How do you know?'

I got a letter. I gave it to him.

He read the letter and said, 'What are you going to do about it, Frank?'

I said "Nothing," and I tore up the letter.

Bob again tried to get Frank to provide a written statement.

Failing that he brought up the subject of Kelsey's partners in crime. As expected, Frank did not budge. Looking at his watch and signaling that it was time to leave by pulling his notes together, Bob asked, kind of *Colombo* style, just one more question:

"I have to leave now and go home. If I work with my son *Peter in the Garden* would that be a good idea?"

Frank responded with the trace of a smile. He later saw Bobby finishing up his trusty work and told him, "That lawyer of yours is one smart guy."

ON KELSEY'S TRAIL

I became restless with the new information, the credible information, that in my mind completely solved the Levi Whiteside murder. But information is not admissible evidence, and that's what we needed for a new trial. I had to do something.

Tommy Montgomery was a Detective in Station B-2 in Roxbury, and the Vice President of the Union. I spoke with him almost daily about union business, and we had become very good friends. He knew all about Bobby Joe's case and did not question our belief in his innocence. Kelsey Reid was seen frequently in Dudley Square which is directly across from the police station, and the area that Tommy patrolled for twenty-five years. Tommy was African American and grew up in the South End. Most everyone in the neighborhood liked and trusted Tommy. Tommy listened to my summary of Kelsey's involvement, and told me he knew him and had arrested him in the past. He would look into it.

A few weeks later Tommy called and gave me this account:

He drove by Kelsey on a side street off the square. He was dirty looking and wearing clothes that he had not changed in days. Tommy edged his detective car, a Crown Victoria, up to Kelsey, put down his window, and trying to use the element of surprise, startled Kelsey with:

"Hey Kelsey. Got a minute to talk about that old man you robbed on Talbot Ave?

He told me, 'I didn't shoot nobody.'

Chris. I did not mention any shooting.

I told him, "Kelsey, just remember, there's no statute of limitations for murder."

Chris. You're on to something.

Kelsey was a piece of work. He was a year younger than Bobby Joe and before he was eighteen he was picked up arrests for assault and battery, A and B with a dangerous weapon, breaking and entering in the nighttime and several drunk and disorderly chares. When he was arrested with Gardner for the armed robbery of a liquor store on Boylston St., he was ending a string of similar robberies. Before he tossed the gun he was in a car with James Campbell and one other male who avoided arrest. The unknown male became a gift to our case.

Boston police are bound by a practice that requires the destruction of firearms when criminal cases are completed. The metal is crushed and likely recycled, so that the agents of random violence and instruments of premeditated death are often resurrected as household products. Because the fourth suspect in the Boylston St. liquor store robbery evaded arrest and was never prosecuted, his remained an "open case" and the .22 long barrel pistol was not reincarnated as an iron or a metal lamp. This was good news for Bobby Joe as the gun that possibly caused the death of Levi Whiteside was secured in a Boston Police evidence locker. I retrieved the trial transcript, and confirmed that the medical examiner, Dr. George Curtis identified the ".22 caliber lead, golden spent bullet" that he extracted from Mr. Whiteside's torso which the court admitted into evidence as exhibit 11. Evidence must remain with the court until all appeals are exhausted, then it is returned to the District Attorney.

We just needed to get that bullet from the DA to be tested by Boston's police ballistician. This proved easier said than done.

DEJA VU

In early June we assembled once again in a courtroom in the Suffolk County courthouse, with Assistant District Attorney John Kiernan, Bobby Joe, and his legal team on the first of six hearing days for our motion for a new trial. It was *deja vu all over again*: Judge John Irwin took his familiar elevated place. Bob, Ron, and I settled into our usual seating. Even Bobby Joe had become so familiar to these proceedings that he was allowed to sit in an unsecured area without any chains, although next to a corrections officer.

Bobby Joe recounted the times in prison when other

inmates, including Paul McKenzie, advised him that he was an innocent man. He recited all the facts and circumstances of his arrest, which if believed, would demonstrate that an *impermissible identification process* was used by the Boston police, and wrongly admitted into evidence. We summoned McKenzie and Brimage, who both appeared as witnesses. They testified, expectedly, with vague memories of other inmates discussing the Whiteside murder, but true to the prison code, refused to label Kelsey Reid as the originator. Kathleen Whiteside confirmed the substance of the Bo Burlingham interview and testified that it was the police who wanted her to look at Bobby Joe in the City Hospital parking lot.

Attorney Bill Homans, a lion in the legal community, stated that if he had all the newly discovered information concerning the show-up, he would have moved for a new trial before completing the first appeal in 1972.

Detective Tom Cashman set out the circumstances of sending Brimage a letter in Concord Prison. Brimage had previously told my father, and testified consistently at the hearing, that he approached Kelsey Reid in the Concord Prison yard and showed him the letter. When Kelsey asked him what he was going to do, Brimage ripped the letter into small pieces. Bob McGrath and Joe Murphy each, respectively, introduced into evidence the results of the hypnosis and polygraph test. All of the newly discovered evidence was presented cumulatively with the evidence found or sorted out during the previous hearings, in front of Judge Irwin, as well as the Federal Court. It was also presented in the context of the findings made by Judge Mclaughlin during the trial, and by the Supreme Judicial Court in its 1972 decision.

The standard for awarding a new trial in these circumstances is based on whether there is a substantial risk that a jury hearing the newly discovered evidence would have reached a different conclusion. Even with all of my bias, I could not see a new jury spending more than several hours before returning a verdict of not guilty. From a commonsense perspective, a new trial should be ordered. Confidence does not preclude caution, especially since in the Leaster case, common sense did not always prevail.

Judge Irwin closed the hearing and told us that he would issue a written decision.

Chapter Six

ONE MORE PUNCH IN THE GUT

John Kiernan was the head of the Suffolk County Homicide Unit when he took over the Leaster case. He was skilled in the courtroom, but more importantly, was ethical and a stand-up guy in all his dealings, personal and professional. More than once he told me, with paternal pride, that he would take his kids' phone calls no matter where he was or what he was doing. This was before smart phones and ubiquitous texting. He did it because he wanted his seven kids to know there was nothing more important than them. He also showed great respect and a hint of affection for Big Bob. So, while we fought for everything we got, there was never a cross word, or a sarcastic aside such as "I guess you believe all your clients are innocent," which regrettably was a refrain from some of the less experienced prosecutors.

John was a member of the heralded 1968 Harvard football team when they faced the nationally recognized rival, and overwhelming favorite, Yale, at the historic fall classic. Alumni from all over the country, indeed the world, return to Cambridge or New Haven for *The Game*. As expected, Yale took an early lead, and with just 42 seconds remaining, and 16 points behind, Harvard miraculously evened the score. Elated, the Harvard team celebrated and would not leave the field for an hour as the dejected Yale quickly departed. The next morning the *Harvard Crimson* headline announced the score of its most famous football game:

HARVARD BEATS YALE 29-29,

John had nothing more to prove in life so he could afford to be a good guy.

~

A few days after Labor Day that year, I was rousted from a sound sleep at 3:00 in the morning. The Detective's Union president, Dan Mahoney, phoned me about a fatal police shooting in the Back Bay and told me to get right over to District 4. When I arrived at the nineteenth century stationhouse that could be a setting for every Sam Spade movie, or more recently, the *Hill Street Blues* television series, I was met with more than a dozen detectives who were involved in a city-wide stolen car chase that ended with a Cadillac driven into the front steps of a row house on Haviland Ave, and the driver, Elijah Pate, a nineteen-year-old Black man lying in the street with five bullets in his body. The detectives were all ordered to file incident reports.

Like every "sudden unattended death," the District Attorney was statutorily required to investigate it. This is a uniform practice for all possible homicides. In such cases, the DA oversees the investigation by the Boston Police Department Homicide Unit. For obvious reasons, this case could not follow that practice. This investigation, like every police deadly force case, could lead to charges, from administrative disciplinary actions to Civil Rights violations and possibly criminal indictments. The officers had the right to counsel before anyone from Internal Affairs of the DA's office spoke to them That counsel was me, and it was the first time I had to respond to a crisis of this magnitude. My immediate task was to interview all of them and then guide them through a police investigation, from that morning through an inquest, and a civil suit several years later. The DA assigned John Kiernan to handle the investigation.

Mayor Kevin White did not seek reelection to what would have been his fifth four-year term, and Boston was in the final days of a tough primary fight for the first open seat for the most powerful position in Boston in decades. The Elijah Pate case dominated the news and the political debates. The outrage of the public, especially the minority community, was immediate and vocal. The public and some of the candidates called for independent investigations, the immediate firing of the detectives, and the creation of Citizen Review Boards. From some angry community activists, there were claims of police assassinations. It was difficult terrain for this not-yet-tested Detective's Union lawyer.

I learned that lots of air and light were the best responses to this and any kind of public crisis. Within days, District Attorney Newman Flanagan ordered an inquest, targeting three detectives who had fired their service revolvers. This is a process where evidence is presented to a judge who decides whether enough evidence exists to present the case to a Grand Jury. Boston Municipal Court Judge George O'Toole was assigned the case and after many days of hearing from witnesses and reviewing other evidence issued a decision.

The Berklee School of Music is a block from the scene,

and many of its students had apartments on Haviland St. It was a warm evening and there were a few rooftop parties going on when the crash and shooting occurred, and some of those students became witnesses. They recalled the timing of the shots using their favorite musical instruments to demonstrate: horn blowers would "toot" out the sound of shots; percussionists would tap them out on the wood of the witness stand. What was interesting was that not one witness could accurately recall the number of shots fired. One student channeled the famed Buddy Rich as he drummed out a machine gun volley. The medical examiner, accident reconstructionist, and the Boston Police investigators were able to provide that number.

When the facts came out, Judge O'Toole wrote a detailed summary of the evidence supporting his conclusion that no criminal action was warranted. The ballistic evidence demonstrated that each of the five bullets that entered Mr. Pate's back and leg were fired as he jumped out of the stolen car after hitting and injuring one detective while he was in reverse doing a "Y" turn, then speeding forward to two detectives who were in front of the car, and in imminent danger. The shooting, though tragic, was justified.

The Inquest decision, a state Attorney General's investigation, and a subsequent civil trial absolved the police of any liability.

During the inquest I ran into John at a nearby pub. The Publik House on Beacon Street had been a meeting place for lawyers and court employees since my friend Michael "Bo" Brodigan opened it in 1973. I sat with John who soon lamented his role in investigating "guys, good guys I've worked with, that I've known for years." And then he shook his head and said, "How strange is this–today you're defending all the cops I'm investigating for violating the rights of a Black kid, and next week, I'm trying to keep a Black man in jail that you and your father say the cops wrongfully arrested." It was a "Go figure!" moment.

When Judge Irwin's decision came down on January 5, 1984, I was angry, upset and extremely disappointed. I was not surprised.

I picked up a copy of the decision on my way to the airport for a previously scheduled weekend in Florida. I was going to cruise on a boat owned by a friend, Richie Hayes, who had shipped it south for the winter. Richie was a top gun in the Massachusetts

Defenders Committee, the state-wide public defender agency. He knew everything about the Leaster case as he had advised me almost from the beginning of the appeals. I told him that Bob, Ron, myself and all the others were tired of not being taken seriously, and that the courts just wanted us to go away.

I had earlier spoken with one of the administrative clerks at the SJC when I was filing papers, who startled me with this broadside: "You know, everybody up here loves your dad, but sometimes enough is enough. There's lots of frivolous appeals being filed. It would be a shame if Bob was made an example, or he was sanctioned."

I took that statement with a laugh, as stupid gossip. Later, I became livid.

"Richie," I told him, "They think we're all nice guys and everything, but just looney zealots." We needed some institutional help. Before I got the request out of my mouth. Richie committed the Mass Defenders to join our next appeal to the SJC.

A few weeks later Bob made the same kind of request to the National College of Criminal Defense Lawyers and Public Defenders. We had both attended, at different times, a ten-day intensive criminal defense course they sponsored at the University of Houston. He was voted 'class president,' not just because he was the oldest among them, but because he organized a side trip to New Orleans. He reached out to his contacts in that organization who had a memory of his formidable lawyer skills, and they promptly agreed to file an Amicus Curiae brief with ours. When it filed its *Friend of the Court* motion to join us, it stated:

> *The association is concerned that the desire in our judicial systems to achieve finality of criminal convictions is overshadowing the primary obligation to see that justice is done.*

At last, the efforts of these *looney zealots* were validated. The assistance of the Mass Defenders and the National College were as critical to our spirits as they were to Bobby's case.

CATCHING OUR BREATH

We all went to work to file an appeal. Like the last one, we needed the "Gate Keeper" approval of a Single Justice before we could be heard by the full bench of the Supreme Judicial Court. We had to convince that single Justice that our appeal presented "a new and substantial question which ought to be determined by the full court."

In early spring Bob and I appeared in front of Paul Liacos, Chief Justice of the Massachusetts Supreme Judicial Court. The tall, thin, and angular man entered the courtroom from behind a velvet curtain, that parted with great solemnity, where he took the middle of seven seats aligned with a crescent shaped bench. He was a warm and gracious gentleman to those who knew him. He intimidated the crap out of me, as he was the number one judge for the entire Massachusetts Court System. He was also known as an expert on evidence. He authored the Massachusetts Handbook on Evidence, popularly known as the *Liacos* book. If an evidence question came up, the prepared lawyer simply cited, *Liacos.* He also did not suffer fools gladly.

What's new since the last time you were here? Liacos asked pointedly.

This was the fast ball pitch that we had been waiting for since 1977. During many pained discussions with friends and colleagues about this case, I often illustrated the volume of exculpatory evidence by raising my hand over a table or a flat surface. "Here's the evidence used at the trial" I would say elevating my hand several inches above the table. "This is what we discovered when we first took the appeal" and I would raise it 10 or 12 inches higher. "And this is how much evidence we have now, if we can ever get it in front of a jury." and I would raise my hand several feet above the office desk or tavern or nightclub bar, as the circumstances dictated.

Bob hit the ball out of the park. His voice always had that magical tone that grabbed interest and attention. In precise terms, and with powerful argument, he told Liacos that a manifest injustice had occurred. It also became obvious that the Chief Justice was thoroughly familiar with all of the details set out in our brief. He questioned both sides about the evidence in the trial, and all the evidence and arguments produced in all the later proceedings.

The case was taken under advisement.

On May 10th telephone calls from 44 Bromfield Street were dispatched throughout Boston.

Judge Liacos had allowed our motion, and the appeal would be heard by the full bench. This was the first time in thirteen years, since the date of Bobby's conviction, that the word *allowed* was paired with any of his pleadings. The decision stood for a whole lot more than its bottom line: Liacos' sixteen-page decision echoed our arguments. He wrote:

> "the new evidence thus bears not only on the questions whether the out-of-court and in-court identifications should have been suppressed, but also on the question whether there is a substantial risk that if the identifications had been admitted but the circumstances of the first identification fully brought out, the jury would have reached a different conclusion."

The Single Justice decision would be the core of our brief to the full bench.

A celebration was in order, and the group that congregated first at the Littlest Bar moved down the street to the fashionable Maison Robert.

JUSTICE FOR JUVENILES

Working Bobby's case was a constant exercise, but not a daily one. I was also going to court and to hearings for hundreds of clients who expected my dedicated professional attention, and mostly received it. For 25 years I represented accused felons of every stripe; those charged and sometimes convicted or exonerated of murder; young and old caught up in the gun and drug activities that challenged or ruined their lives; and not otherwise bad people who drank too much or acted very stupidly. I also negotiated dozens of contracts for police, probation and court officers, and spent hours with Police Detectives who faced disciplinary hearings for everything from rules and regulations violations to perjury, excessive force, civil rights claims and criminal indictments. When my boat needed repairs or I fell behind on a tuition payment, I would take on an unpleasant divorce, or agree to represent a very demanding client.

One of my most memorable cases from those thousands involved Mark Devlin.

Juvenile justice in Massachusetts and most of the country was barbaric through the mid- twentieth century. As a kid I knew about places like "Lyman" and "Shirley" and other reform schools, but I never met anyone who was sent to them. That is, until the spring of 1984, when I received an interesting phone call from a friend, Peter O'Malley.

Peter was a well-known operator within the literary world of Cambridge and Boston. He co-founded Ploughshares, a magazine that published rising poets and writers. It was named after his Central Square Irish Bar, the Plough and Stars. He composed music, although he never played an instrument. One opus was my wedding composition; another was a requiem for my father.

Peter asked me to help a writer whose memoir, *Stubborn Child,* had received rave reviews and was set for publication and a book tour. But there was a glitch: the author had an open case for armed robbery.

Mark Devlin lived a tortured childhood. His father assaulted the oldest child unmercifully, throwing him against walls and strapping him. His mother, overwhelmed by five other children, a drunk husband, and poverty, stood by helplessly. Neighbors who witnessed the abuse notified the authorities who investigated and found that Mark had no structure, stayed away from home and was unmanageable. They noted that he periodically defecated in the sink. Family Services urged his mother to take out a juvenile court complaint, telling her that it would give Mark the structure and training that he desperately required. Mark's unfortunate journey began because his mother trusted them.

Mark was brought before a judge in the Boston Juvenile Court who declared him delinquent as a *stubborn child* and who *sentenced* the seven-year-old boy, barely out of the toddler age, to the Lyman Reform School. Mark was raised in a jail setting until he was sixteen. The first chapter of his book describes how a correction officer slammed shut the metal door of his room, a "cell," and told him to stop crying or he would get ten inches of his shoe leather shoved up his ass.

In the early seventies a juvenile reform movement took hold in Massachusetts under the direction of Jerome Miller, a state official. He closed the infamous detention centers and reshaped the philosophy of juvenile treatment. Notably, delinquency was no longer a crime, and the goal was no longer punishment, but providing services.

During my first days at the Malden District Court, I took on a caseload of juvenile clients. They were ones who were charged, not in criminal complaints, but in various *petitions*: Care and Protection because of parental abuse or neglect; Child in Need of Services, brought on by truancy, or that proverbial *stubborn-ness*, or being unmanageable at home or in school; and of course, *delinquency*, a catchall for every kind of otherwise criminal conduct from shoplifting to murder.

My introduction to this session included a brief sidebar conference with the most gentlemanly judge I had met, John Ligotti, who asked me, and I quote from memory, "Brother Muse, do you have street sense?" When I told him I had earlier taught at East Boston High, his hometown, I received a thumbs up.

I approached this stage of lawyering guided by the wisdom of Father Flanagan, the priest at Boy's Town, made famous in a black and White movie starring Spencer Tracy who regularly intoned, "there is no such thing as a bad boy." So, while I still had a piss and vinegar approach to fighting charges against my adult clients, here, with young kids, my goal was to get services and support. Mark Devlin was a casualty to a time when incarceration with ten inches of shoe leather up the rectum was the prescription for rehabilitating wayward youth.

The one redeeming feature of Mark's incarceration was that he defeated loneliness with books. He read everything he could get his hands on. The Perry Mason series was a favorite. He used to insist he was my peer because of those readings. So, literature guided him to the Literati: Mark's brilliant mind was recognized by writers in Cambridge, and by Peter O'Malley who met Mark at his literary salon/Irish bar. They nurtured his writing and subsidized his modest expenses as he was homeless, or as he described himself, a "Road Scholar." When Peter contacted me, the galleys of his book had been circulated and *Stubborn Child was* ready for the presses.

Almost ten years before, Mark was indicted for the armed robbery of a Harvard Square restaurant. Peter O'Malley asked me to help clean up this case as soon possible, so he was not arrested on a warrant while he was on the book tour.

I went right to work. I got a copy of the indictment and met with the Assistant District Attorney to arrange for Mark to turn himself in and to get him released. Jay Carney had the case which was now in Middlesex Superior Court. Later, he became a highly regarded and well-known criminal defense lawyer whose clients included James Bulger, known by law enforcement as Whitey. He also became a very good friend. I took the police report, reviewed it, and noted that the victim who was bound and blindfolded, could not see (and, I therefore assumed, could not identify) the third individual who was merely present at the restaurant, and who the Commonwealth claimed was my client.

Now, if anyone knew identification law, well, that would be me. We put the case over for arraignment and discussed possible plea options. I told Jay about Mark's horrid life before the laws changed the juvenile justice system, what I thought was an otherwise clean record, and with dumb bravado, told him his case was weak.

Mark was a gentle and likable soul. His story was heartbreaking, and like his friends in Cambridge, my family and I took him in like a stray puppy. Big Bob took him under his wing and brought him down to his summer house on Buzzards Bay for a week of pre summer cleanup. Mark said in a *Globe Magazine* feature story, "For the first time in my life, I [felt] a part of a family and I [had] a sense of well-being. They've sort of adopted me."

Mark gave me a little history surrounding the indictment. He met some guys in the Combat Zone who were thieves. He tried to impress them by explaining how they could rob a restaurant where he had worked, describing layout and where the money was kept. They told him he was required to join them if he wanted his cut. The robbery was successful, until the two main culprits were caught. Mark was indicted and defaulted without appearing in court. He was roaming the streets of Boston and Cambridge, and police and prosecutors lost interest in pursuing that very minor player.

During this time, Mark suggested I read the draft of his book. I declined; I was too busy. He pushed the idea, in fact, he became insistent: "I really think you should read my book." I relented.

His story was gripping and powerful, beginning with how a guard slammed the steel door shut on the seven-year-old delinquent. The next few pages recounted his lonely and dysfunctional life in Jamaica Plain near Franklin Field. Mid-way through the book I learned he was sent to a federal prison in Virginia for interstate theft of an automobile, where he spent three years. So much for a clean record. Then, a confession: Mark laid out in specific detail how he participated in the restaurant robbery as an accomplice. So much for a challenge to the unreliable ID.

A speedy trial is a constitutional right: For Mark it was an urgent, NASCAR speed. Jay asked to read Mark's biography, just to learn more about the person who might get probation. I put him off, saying the galley proofs were confidential. Then when I learned the publication date was approaching, I hit the accelerator. When Jay offered a suspended sentence, I jumped. However, he wanted to thoroughly investigate his record. I quickly offered up his federal conviction. He wanted to explore probation conditions. "He's an alcoholic, he'll go to AA, he'll get a job…he'll do everything you want. Let's move this case along, Jay!"

Mark pled guilty, Jay went through with the deal, as the criminal justice system worked for Mark, at last. The book came out later and was well received. The director of the French Connection optioned the book for a movie. Mark went on all the talk shows, in Boston and cities in all the big TV markets. He was very polished. I appeared on the *Good Morning America* show with him, and he patted my arm and told me to relax as the cameras rolled. He was written up in national magazines. Harry Reasoner came to my office to interview Mark for *60 Minutes*. However, his producer dropped the segment in the middle of filming because Mark's mother refused to go on screen, and I declined to cajole her to do so.

But, after every interview, with all the adulation he received, he went back to his home on the streets. From time to time, he would get arrested, and my brother Pete or I would straighten things out. He made valiant but always failed attempts to get sober. He called me once and excitedly told me he was diagnosed as bipolar.

"And why was this good news?"

"It explains why I'm an alkie. I can take drugs and fix it."

Mark was involuntarily hospitalized several times for the next ten years of his life. Treatment was sometimes too little, and often too much. To his credit, Mark never lost his fighting spirit, especially against institutions that held him in custody.

Once, he sent me a copy of a letter of protest to the administrator of a hospital where he had been committed, claiming they had violated his right to treatment. Here, it was because he wet his bed and they would not change his sheets or give him clean pajamas.

"And I will speak to my lawyer who has been a Superior

Court Judge in Brockton for two years. His sister is a judge and his mother a probate judge. Two of his brothers are trial attorneys, and together they have the south shore locked up. Please remand and notify these Nazi-like tactics of the graveyard shift."

He still had a piss and vinegar fight in him when it came to personal dignity.

Mark never recovered from his childhood or his juvenile incarcerations. Those demons came back too often to haunt him. He took his own life with pills in a Braintree hotel room on March 10, 2005, two months after sending me that complaint.

There were no burial plans for Mark, so Big Bob made one as I was bedridden with pneumonia, and my brother Peter stood in for me. With great effort he finally located Mark's mother to tell her about his death, so that she could attend her son's service with members of the Muse family.

People still read the book of this "useless street person" as Mark saw himself. Juvenile justice remains a work in progress. In the past decade, the courts have recognized that the development of a child's brain goes through pronounced stages of organic growth, sometimes reflected during the early years, in recklessness, impulsivity, immaturity and lack or responsibility. This has been obvious to parents of teenagers for generations as an explanation for general misbehavior.

It became an issue of legal significance when the U. S. Supreme Court found it unconstitutional to impose the death penalty on juveniles, and later, when the court eliminated the denial of parole opportunities to juveniles given life sentences. The essence of their reasoning was that a juvenile's criminal conduct during that brain development phase could not forecast his behavior as an adult, and hence, it was cruel and unusual to sentence him as though an adult. Creative alternatives to incarceration such as Restorative Justice, emphasis on family counseling and direct services to the offender are taking the place of automatic detention. Mark's book is still in circulation and read by juvenile justice advocates who continue try to make a difference.

Bobby Joe and Mark spent many years in cruel prisons. Mark never had the love and guidance of parents and siblings to create a strength within himself. He was damaged from birth. His contrast with Bobby Joe need not be drawn. The lessons from each are obvious.

ON THE ROPES AGAIN

Bob and I looked smart, or *smaht*, in our "sincerity blue" suits as we awaited our turn to argue on the thirteenth floor of the Suffolk County courthouse, before five Justices of the Supreme Judicial Court. Liacos could not participate because of a procedural rule. But we knew he was there, if not in spirit, at least as a substantial footnote.

The argument went predictably, and the exchanges were cordial. When asked to sum up his position on the case, Bob referenced and repeated the contents of Bobby Joe's pro-se petition for Habeas Corpus which Bobby, with assistance from Victor, filed in 1977

Respectfully on new Habeas Corpus petition raised—illegal identification by the alleged wife of the alleged victim- the supreme court has dealt with this form of unconstitutional identification in united states v. wade, 388us218, (1967) wherein on the night of the so-called murder this defendant was walking the street: police without probable cause illegally arrested defendant. was taken by policeman to the victim's house and the victim's wife was brought out, to car by policeman, while the policeman pointed his finger at this defendant, saying "ain't that him. This form of random capricious arrest is shocking to the conscious of justice of our great country constitution and to the rights of free men; wherein your petitioner pray for relief.

We were closing the circle started in March 1977 and coming back to our beginning.

Neither one of us was in a hurry to get back to the office. It was Bobby Joe's 35th birthday, so we decided to get a cake and visit him in Bay State. We walked to the North End, near my condo, and when we told the salesgirl at Mike's Pastry that we were bringing the cake to a prison, "so can you give us a large enough one to hold a file." she first laughed, then knocked a few dollars off the price when she was told the true circumstances of our visit. "I have a boyfriend who went to jail for a time," she explained.

Bobby was thrilled to see us, to receive the news of the SJC hearing, and to devour his birthday cake, not necessarily in that order. Later that week I sent "progress reports" to about a dozen friends who regularly expressed interest in Bobby's slow march to justice.

One was sent to Bill Dougherty, a financial guy, and a close friend of Supreme Court Justice William Brennan who authored the seminal *United States v. Wade* identification case. I wrote to Billy that his friend's ears should be ringing because we extensively quoted that case in our brief and oral argument

For the next few days, we felt a gradually dissipating euphoria. As the months added up without a decision we grew restless and nervous, trying to read the delay as a positive sign.

Then it happened. Again.

On June 6th, 1985, I was attending a conference put on by the Society for Missing and Exploited Children. It was a happy occasion: I had been asked to speak to a group in Providence Rhode Island about my involvement in locating the two sons of Karen Ring Fitzpatrick, who had been abducted by their father.

Sometime in 1982 my sister- in- law Debbie approached me about helping out someone with whom Debbie had been working at the Kennedy library. She had become good friends with Doris Kearns Goodwin, the noted historian and author. Doris was friends with Karen Fitzpatrick, who was heartbroken over the abduction of her children by her ex-husband who was disappointed with a custody order. Could I help?

Karen cooked for the Goodwins in their Concord home. Soon after getting involved, I saw Doris on a local Sunday morning news show on the last week of December. She and the other panelists were asked to share their New Year's wishes. She instantly replied that she prayed that "her best friend Karen get her kids back." I thought it was extraordinary that someone as famous as Doris, who was friends with presidents and national leaders, would have such affection for someone who provided household help. This was before I read her famous *Wait 'til Next Year,* her memoir about her middle-class upbringing on Long Island when the Dodgers broke everyone's heart, especially those of Doris and the dad that she adored. She was raised and remained a good, basic, and kindhearted person. When her best friend needed help, she gave it.

When I met Karen, I found a tough and equally kindhearted woman. There was no weeping, just purpose and persistence. Against the opinions of a few investigators whom she hired, I advised Karen to go full bore publishing her kids' abduction. If her ex-husband, a native of Ireland, learned she was tracking him, so what! Also, knowing Karen, he would have assumed it. Posters went up everywhere, from telephone poles to milk cartons. I used whatever contacts I had to assist her, and when a big break occurred, I addressed the legal details to get her kids back.

In late June 1984 Karen was told that Interpol had located her kids in Cardiff, Wales. A local schoolteacher had viewed the closing clip of the Adam Walsh video, a movie about an abducted child in Florida. At the end of the video, pictures of approximately 50 abducted kids were shown. The teacher who rented the video recognized Sean and Eddie to be students in a Cardiff elementary school. It made great sense: It was a short ferry ride to the Irish coast.

Doris, her husband Dick, and I made plans to retrieve the kids. I thought it would be helpful to get an introduction to the American embassy in London, in case we ran into any red tape.

Doris, the chronicler of the Kennedys, had an easy task obtaining a support letter from Senator Ted Kennedy. I called my friends at House Speaker Tip O'Neill's office for the same. For extra measure, Doris secured the intervention of Congressman Jim Shannon. They each wrote detailed letters of support to our Ambassador to St. James Court, with a request for every assistance they could provide. I drove to the Cambridge Probate Court and expedited a certified copy of the custody award to Karen found in their divorce decree. Karen and I boarded planes for London.

After our arrival, we met with the social worker who had taken custody of the kids. She had the gentle manner of a librarian in an Agatha Christie murder mystery. She insisted we enter the Old Bailey Court through its security entrance with police assistance. "You can't be too careful with those Irish, you know." I acknowledged her concern, feeling a virtual kick in my ass from my one-generation-removed daughter of County Roscommon mother. On July 4th, a judge with a sense of humor gave the kids their "independence" from their irresponsible dad. We journeyed back to the USA and were greeted with a roomful of national and local press. It was a heady time.

In Providence, I waited to be called to the podium to talk about the courage of Karen and the joy of finding the kids. Before my scheduled time, I stepped out of the auditorium to telephone my office. My secretary Josephine could not hide some kind of bad news. She quietly and quickly told me that the SJC had issued its decision. "It's not good." she said.

"Let me speak to my father…"

"He's with someone." she answered.

"Let me talk to him… go interrupt him " I demanded.

Bob spoke into the phone with a broken voice, and most assuredly teary eyes. His sobs were those of a strong man and sounded like the clearing of his throat or his nose. But they were sobs.

I listened to his brief synopsis of our defeat. He told me that the court wrote a decision that was foreign to the facts of our case but would be difficult to overturn; in fact, impossible to overturn.

The auditorium folks were paging me. I tried to cheer Bob up before I departed. I described for him the scene out of the movie Animal House when John Belushi and others were expelled from the university by the dean. Paraphrasing Bluto I said: "Shit Bob, 8 years of college down the drain." I then added, "I'm sorry. I love you."

I went into the auditorium wearing a happy-face mask.

I did not get my chance to grieve until about nine o'clock that night. I met my girlfriend Joan at the Sail Loft bar and restaurant on the waterfront. I railed against the court, the justices of the

SJC in particular, and threatened to rip up my lawyer's bar card, as Joan patiently listened, and I angrily got drunk. I repeated my thoughts and my venom until closing time. When I woke the next morning, my head was the size of a very large basketball. I arrived at the office, late, and in a foul mood. It was not until I sat down that I noticed the 12 by 18 photo of John Belushi, wearing a sweat-shirt marked *College*.

On a scrap of legal pad paper, scotch taped to the picture, was the notation in my father's handwriting:

"To the SJC: We have not yet begun to fight."

My laughing almost broke the blood vessels which were throbbing in my head.

THE ERROR

I did not have the stomach to see Bobby Joe right away.

My father went to Bay State within a day of receiving the decision, and each consoled the other. Bob said that our client took the news without bitterness, just regret. He told him that he would file a motion for reconsideration with the SJC. I forget whether he expressed any hope of reversal. I was so angry with the court that I could not bring myself to read the decision. I scanned it for sure and gleaned the general holdings and the bottom line. I did not expect any relief from the courts. I considered them a failure and I blocked any discussion about the details of the decision. The first time I read it with any degree of attention was in 2016 when I participated in a conference of lawyers and judges on the topic of Wrongful Convictions.

The day after my hangover, I walked up to the state house and obtained a copy of commutation guidelines issued by the Governor to the Advisory Board of Pardons. Commutation is a process whereby the Governor reduces the crime of first-degree murder to second degree. Second degree murderers are eligible for parole after 15 years of incarceration. While it is an extraordinary remedy, it was one which inmates with exceptional prison records, and with demonstrated potential to make it outside the walls, could obtain. I did not have a clue about what the Advisory Board of Pardons was, or how one made an application. But I had a plan: I would speak to and learn from one who did.

Three days after the decision I drove to Bay State. I had

previously scheduled periodontal surgery earlier in the day and my mouth was still swollen, and my gums still bleeding. I had no idea how invasive it was, thinking I would get Novocain that would wear off. I had to stop several times by the side of the road to spit out the accumulated blood in my mouth. I had told Bobby to expect me, and I was not going to let this unanticipated medical and dental annoyance stop me.

I hugged Bobby when I first saw him. We walked outdoors in the back area which bordered the Norfolk Prison grounds with the monstrous browning concrete fortress in the distance. We said very little in the beginning.

What happened? Bobby finally asked.

"The Supreme Judicial Court said you got a fair trial." I answered.

A fair trial, they said I got a fair trial….how the hell did I get a fair trial if I am innocent.

I started to rant. My swollen mouth and the bloodletting made me look and sound mean and nasty.

" I know you are fuckin' innocent…you know you are fuckin innocent…everybody who has worked on this case knows you're fuckin innocent. I don't give a fuck if the Supreme Judicial Court doesn't think you're fuckin innocent. Everybody in the world will know that you're fuckin innocent… and you're gonna get out of here. You're gonna get your freedom."

How am I getting my freedom?

"Commutation." I answered.

Now he got angry.

I can't get any commutation. It takes 20 years of jail time just to get a hearing. Just about everybody here in Bay State is doing a life bit. Everybody is looking for a commutation. I won't get a commutation until I'm old. I'll never have a family.

He calmed down as he realized how agitated he had become.

I know you're trying to help me, but I'll be too old to have a family by the time I get a commutation. he said softly. *Besides, I can't get a commutation unless I say I'm sorry. I'm not going to say I'm sorry for a crime I did not commit,* he added emphatically

I conceded the obvious. "I'm sure you know more about it than me. Let me look into it. But I know we're at least going to try."

I was concerned about how Bobby was going to handle this last defeat. Frankly, I was worried that he would give up the hope that sustained us all.

"You have every right to, but don't get angry Bobby. I'm angry…Bob's angry. We will be angry for you. You don't need to be angry if we are angry for you."

I know what you're getting at Chris. Don't worry I'm going to be fine. I just need a little   time. But I'll be fine.

Chapter Seven

NEVER HAVING TO SAY YOU'RE SORRY

I went back to look at the commutation guidelines. Bobby was right: A pre-condition for it is a demonstration of remorse. This would be a problem.

I learned that the Massachusetts Parole Board served as the Advisory Board of Pardons. I had a friend, Mike Albano from Springfield, who had been a member for several years. I contacted him at the Parole Board office, and we agreed to meet at the Publik House.

So one day after work in July, in a back booth, Mike gave me the soup- to- nuts lesson in pleading a case before the Board.

"What about 'lack of remorse' as an issue?" I asked.

"This would be a problem, it has been dealt with in the past, and the board is very skeptical of these kinds of claims. If a convict cannot come to grips with his crime, and take responsibility for his actions, he generally is not a good candidate for parole." He explained that I would have to be prepared to argue that Bobby's claim of innocence was reasonable and should not be a bar.

Mike advised me to begin to assemble his institutional record, and to make definite plans for a job and housing. I would need a lot of support from his family and community, and anyone that interacted favorably with him in prison.

That might get me a favorable commutation decision. Then the real battle would be with the Governor, and the Governor's Council. If there is any controversy, for instance outrage from the victim's family or opposition from the district attorney, then there would be problems. He advised me to get favorable public support. In order to get that kind of support, I would need publicity. These were political decisions and public support was crucial.

Mike was an excellent instructor. I made a mental note of every point he made. Probably the most important information was the name, and an introduction to Joyce Hooley, the Parole Board's Executive Director. I filed Bobby's petition on August 9th, and for the next eight months I bugged Joyce incessantly.

I learned that it was fairly routine for the Board to deny the first request for a hearing. This would set the application process back by a year. There was probably a sound administrative reason for this practice: applicants should be patient, and the board should review most applications several times before formally deciding them. I felt that Bobby's was the exceptional case, and a hearing should be given on his first application. His claim that he would not get out of prison in time to have a family haunted me.

I called up Mike Albano. He said to come over to the Board *now*, and I could speak to other Board members to make my pitch. I pulled a file together and fast-walked to the Saltonstall office building where I met with Mike and two other board members. I laid out the case, and when the issue of remorse came up, I showed them the Judge Liacos decision for the proposition that at least one SJC Justice thought Bobby deserved a new trial. If a Supreme Court Justice saw possible error in Bobby's conviction, Bobby's protestation of innocence was not off base, and his lawyer's claims were not frivolous.

Gradually Mike's office filled with three more members. Each grilled me on one aspect of the case or the other. All my responses were sound. The members were direct, sometimes skeptical, but always sincere and empathetic. I knew that freeing a first-degree murder convict was a profound decision. I respected the personal responsibility they brought to the task.

Unlike the courts, the Board was not adversarial. If Bobby deserved commutation, they wanted to give it to him. The standards were strict, and the process daunting, but if he deserved it, he would get it. There were no egos; there was no gamesmanship. They would get back to me with a hearing date decision.

I walked with a skip back to my office. I called Mike to express my thanks and appreciation to him, and to all of my new best friends on the Parole Board. And then I got back to work.

SERENDIPITY

I was walking to work one morning, when one block from Quincy Market, I saw Bo Burlingham coming from the opposite direction. We had kept in touch, and I knew that he was heading to his waterfront office where he was Executive Editor of INC. Magazine. He asked me about Bobby Joe. His cheerful smile told me I had all morning to speak to him about an important thing on my mind. So I updated Bo; first the depressingly bad news from the SJC, and then the commutation we were attempting. I recounted my conversation with Mike Albano and explained how important favorable publicity was to get the job done.

Bo had always believed in the innocence of Bobby Joe, and it was not necessary to ask for Bo's help more than once. He told me he still had contacts at the *Boston Globe*, and he had frequently mentioned the facts and circumstances of the Leaster story to editors. He put more spring to my step when Bo emphasized that this was the time to push for press coverage. He made it happen when Charles Kenney, a reporter with the *Boston Globe Magazine*, was assigned the story.

Charlie was two or three years younger than me and had attended Catholic Memorial High School in the same class as my brother Stephen. He spent several hours with me, then with my father, and learned the history of the case, and the names of people who were involved in it in one way or another. He had other assignments to complete before he could go deeply into Bobby's story. He promised to attend the commutation hearing. I had pestered Joyce Hooley at least twice a week at the parole board with my inquiries of the hearing date. At long last the notification was sent; March 31, 1986

I did exactly as I was told. I prepared witnesses to demonstrate to the board that the claim of innocence was a reasonable one, and that Bobby's refusal to express remorse, to say he was sorry for a crime he did not commit, should not bar their consideration.

Bo Burlingham described the depth of research he conducted while freelancing a story for the *Globe*. Every witness, all the lawyers, some of the jurors, and even the trial judge, Walter Mclaughlin were interviewed. He spoke to family members in Boston and Alabama. In the middle of his research, he became so convinced of Bobby's innocence that he lost his objectivity as a journalist. That is why, he told the board, the story was never completed for publication.

Bill Homans, generously described by his biographer Mark S. Brodin, as "a criminal lawyer of great genius. A civil libertarian. A hero and role model for a generation of lawyers", explained how this case of possible mistaken identification occurred. With his easy but clear spoken manner he was nonetheless adamant that if all the newly discovered evidence of the circumstances of the identification were known by him at the time of drafting the first appeal, he would have moved for a new trial in front of Judge Mclaughlin, and he believed he would have received one.

"But why did not the SJC grant him one in its most recent decision?" he was asked.

" The SJC is an admirable court" he stated diplomatically, "but the decision to overrule a trial judge in these cases is unusual, because they must find clear error." That did not mean that his appeal lacked credibility, he explained.

Richie Hayes, a lifelong resident of South Boston, with a healthy fighting attitude not uncommon for the neighborhood he never left, talked about his twelve years with the Mass Defenders. He recalled his first assignment in the Dorchester District Court in the early seventies:

"I was doing 4 to 12 cases like the Talbot hold-up every day, five days a week. Drugs were so rampant, our office developed drug rehabilitation alternatives. Addicts were robbing mom and pop stores every day."

He indicated that every one of his clients had a rap sheet of other offenses before they were charged with armed robbery: handbag snatching, drug possession, juvenile offenses, truancy…something. But Bobby Joe had a perfect record.

"I don't know if he did or did not commit that crime. I can tell you that he did not fit the pattern."

Charles Ogletree at the time was a visiting professor at Harvard Law School. He was on the road to a tenured position and a distinguished academic life at Harvard, where he established a nationally recognized criminal law institute, mentored future president Barack Obama, and many others, and authored several books. The professor continued a storied legal career that brought him to the Senate hearing for one of his clients, Anita Hill, and to assorted courtrooms throughout the country for others.

In February he wrote to my father offering his assistance. He had learned of the case from my brother Robert with whom he had worked in Washington D.C.

I took the Red Line to Harvard Square a few weeks later and met "Tree" in a restaurant on Mass. Ave. where I delivered a complete trial transcript, and most of our pleadings. He read everything.

Without any hesitancy, Professor Ogletree told the board that based upon his review of the case, it was his opinion that Bobby Joe Leaster was innocent.

Here was my expert witness!

Brownie Speer ran the appellate division of the Mass. Defenders. His reputation was stellar, and most of the board members either knew him, or just as importantly, knew of him. He was revered by all the lawyers he mentored, assisted, or simply shared space with him at the Mass. Defenders. He could have walked out their door and made a fortune writing appellate briefs for law firms that printed money. He was happiest in his cluttered office and writing brilliantly for the indigent defendants who never knew how lucky they were.

I will never forget the words he carefully chose to urge the board to ignore the requirement of remorse:

"I have reviewed Bobby's case, and I can assure you that his insistence on his innocence is not a stubborn one."

Looking back, I am in awe of the fire power from the legal community that appeared on behalf of Bobby Joe Leaster. But the civilian witnesses were just as important.

Mel Springer, a prison counselor at Norfolk, ran the "Lifer's program." Bobby joined his group soon after his arrival and made a lasting impression.

Mel believed in Bobby's innocence because of his character. He told the Board that this testimonial was something he had never given on behalf of any other inmate.

Bobby's cousin Ruby Thomas described the gentle loving boy she knew in Alabama, who was raised just like a brother to her, and who joined her in Boston in 1969. She described *the worst thing he ever did:* skipping Sunday School. He would never hurt anyone, recalling how he once moved a ladybug off the road "because it had the right to live too."

One pleasant, and impactful, surprise came when Assistant District Attorney Fran O'Meara told the board that his office was confident that Bobby received a fair trial. But, he said, his office took no position on what the Board should do. It was effectively, *commute the sentence if that is what you decide is right.* Few prosecutors would go against the opinions of a murder victim's family. Franny had the balls to do it.

A QUEEN'S GAMBIT

The next day, the *Globe* ran a full story of the hearing in its Metro section. The advice I received from Mike Albano to get the story in front of the public produced one unexpected result: I received a phone call from a man who told me that he had read the article and knew that Bobby Joe was innocent. I persuaded him to come to my office.

The fortyish Black man who insisted that I keep his identity confidential, and who I later identified as "Rob," told me that in 1981 he was paroled after serving twelve years for second degree murder, now had a family and a good job, and did not want any publicity to disrupt it. But he also believed it was not right for a man wrongfully convicted of a crime to have to spend the rest of his life in jail. With my agreement to keep his involvement confidential, he told me what he knew.

In March 1973, he was transferred from Walpole Prison to Norfolk. The following Saturday, he was in a recreation room in the building where new men were processed. A 'new man' entered the room occupied by a half dozen or so inmates. He greeted several that he recognized and stated how glad he was to see them. The atmosphere in the room suddenly changed when the new man pointed to Bobby Joe Leaster and laughed about how Bobby was doing time for something that he himself did-murder.

"Rob" did nothing and began to play chess.

In the middle of his chess game, the new man started ragging Bobby Joe, saying he was in Norfolk for only a short time, and described how good it was on the streets.

"What did you do when you heard this?" I asked.

"I lost my queen."

"You what?"

"I lost my concentration, and I lost my queen."

Rob then told me how he approached Bobby Joe, "and asked him straight out: 'Are you doing time for this guy?'"

When Bobby said *yes,* "Rob" asked if he wanted to see the superintendent or the officer in charge. Bobby replied *no,* his lawyer was handling his appeal. "Rob" explained that going to the superintendent was not being a snitch because the new man brought it out.

Within several weeks I obtained confirmation from "Rob"

that his transfer date was absolutely March 1, 1973. I also learned that Peter Gardner was transferred from Concord to the more restrictive Norfolk for disciplinary reasons on March 2, 1973. March third fell on a Saturday. The story checked out without "Rob" snitching.

CHAMPAGNE

Throughout May and June, I constantly bothered Joyce Hooley about when the decision would be reported. In mid-June I received an update: The Board voted on Bobby's petition and would issue a full written decision soon. She went silent when I asked the vote tally.

I was not going to let her off the phone.

"If you can't tell me the decision, can you at least give me a hint?" I asked.

She declined. I tried a different approach:

"If I were to take my father out to celebrate the issuance of the decision, should I order   champagne or vinegar?" I asked.

Joyce hesitated.

"Come on… all I want to know is what should I drink.."

Silence

"All right. You should order champagne" she finally answered.

I shouted my love and adoration to her into the phone.

"One last question… about the vote… should I order four bottles of champagne or five….or six,,,.?"

"Oh, stop it! Go out and order seven bottles of champagne!"

Wow! A 7-0 unanimous decision

On July 24th I drove to a news distributor in Salem to obtain an advance copy of the *Globe Magazine* with Charlie Kenney's article which would be circulated with the Sunday papers. It was a cover story with a beautiful full-page photo of Bobby. I quickly read and completely digested a sympathetic and persuasive article on Bobby's innocence, that neither Bob nor I could improve. When I called my office with my excited review, I learned that the Parole Board decision was issued, and if I could get into Boston before 5:00, I could get a copy.

I flew into downtown. John Curran, the Chairman, was putting final touches on the decision. He handed it to me and said that the board was truly impressed with the manner in which Bobby conducted himself for the past fifteen years: "If he was guilty, he was a remarkable human being. If he was innocent, (and Curran indicated this also was probable) "then Bobby Joe was awe inspiring."

I kept in telephone contact with my office, and through my secretary decided to meet Bob in a restaurant in Dedham. I already had dinner plans with my new love, Karen Leonard. I picked her up in the Back Bay, to meet up with my father at J.C.Hillary's restaurant and drive out to see Bobby.

I introduced my father to my future bride, and over a beer at the bar we read the magazine article and the decision. We were ecstatic.

We hurried to Bay State before the end of visiting hours. When you enter the facility there is a large room to the immediate right. Bobby met us at the entrance, and we walked with him to a place with several seats. After we summarized the commutation decision and showed Bobby the cover of the Boston Sunday Globe magazine, he knew that he would get released and the world would know he was innocent.

Bobby could not contain himself. One by one the other prisoners came over to congratulate him and us. Some of them just wanted to meet Karen.

Chapter Eight

JUSTICE FOR BOBBY JOE

Charlie Kenney, long before he became a successful author, was first and foremost a reporter who practiced that craft with the highest ideals and best skills of that profession. My father and I dug into the evidence of Bobby Joe's case to marshal the facts to our pre-ordained conclusion to argue before judges and benches of judges that Bobby did not receive a fair trial. Charlie took the same evidence and wrote the narrative that persuaded an entire city that Bobby Joe was innocent. He did it by laboring through documents and interviews, and with his easy prose, convincingly established that justice was not done.

The public reaction to Charlie's article, JUSTICE *FOR BOBBY JOE* was overwhelming. TV stations set up interviews at Bay State and on Bromfield Street. Letters came in from all over, especially from women who fell in love with Bobby's ripped weightlifter's body. The best response came on July 28th from an anonymous caller who later identified himself as Mark Johnson.

Mark had read the magazine article, and as a result called Bob and told his story of that rainy day in 1970 when he was just thirteen years old and living in the vicinity of Talbot Ave. and Mallard Ave.:

> "It was a rainy, drizzly day. I was playing with some friends and while walking through a back lot between Colonial Avenue and Mallard Street, I saw 2 fellows running through the lot like someone was chasing them. One of them was wearing a beret type hat. They ran into Stewey Loughtman's house. Eddie said to me, 'I wonder what they are running for.' We then walked down Mallard Street to go to the store, when Mrs. Whiteside came running out, screaming that 'Levi is dead.' After a while Simmons and I walked back toward the same place we had come from. A cop was walking around when I said, 'They ran into the house.' and then he said to me 'What did you say?' and I said, nothin."

He studied Bobby Joe's arrest photo that was included in the *Globe* article and was certain that neither one of the two men was Bobby Joe Leaster. With a respectful insistence from Bob, Mark agreed to come to the office one day later. He was forthcoming, but nervous and he refused to have his statement recorded.

"No way," he said, "I'd be in deep trouble."

The 28-year-old Boston School teacher described how he was the only one of his childhood group who was not in jail or dead. The neighborhood around the Talbot Variety was drug and crime infested at the time of the robbery. He knew Katherine Whiteside as "Cat" and he sketched the area around the store, marking the streets where he lived and where the actual robbers ran. It was raining when he saw them, and minutes later "Cat" was chasing them and screaming "Levi is dead."

Everything Mark reported ended up in an affidavit that he signed on September 4th, six weeks after his phone call to Bob. During the delay, as Bob encouraged Mark to do the right thing although he was still very nervous, Bob investigated the details of his statement.

Bob checked the weather report for September 27, 1970, which disclosed it was raining. He obtained a Boston Police photo taken after their response to the murder scene which displayed the wet streets. He went to the map room of the Boston Redevelopment Authority and obtained a 1965 aerial photo of the variety store area that confirmed there was a vacant lot between Mallard Street and Colonial Ave. 1970 residence data confirmed the addresses of the people Mark had earlier identified.

Mark reacted to the efforts of Bob to validate his statement and relented. He trusted Big Bob and agreed to go public.

I coordinated television and print interviews. Charlie Austin, who I and many others considered the preeminent TV reporter in Boston, scheduled an interview with Bobby at Bay State. Among all the local reporters, he had the best contacts with the Boston Police who trusted him absolutely. Because of his fairness, Charlie usually got the 'scoop' on murders and other major crimes, and his face was often found below the heading, *Breaking News,* with microphone in hand, as he spoke in front of yellow crime scene tape on the very tough streets of Boston. I was honored to be called his friend.

I watched this African American's interaction with Bobby. When he finished his filmed interview, I walked with Charlie to the parking lot and talked. He was visibly moved by what Bobby said and how he said it. I forget his exact words, but it was something like, "It is just not fair."

Charlie was preparing to leave with his cameraman, when he learned the Channel 4 truck had broken down. He asked if he could ride back to the city with me so he could get the tape on air for the noontime edition. "Oh yes," I thought, "I'll be able to tell you the whole story." For the next hour Charlie learned every positive detail of our saga. When he got out of my car, visibly shaken by the full story, I knew I had a convert, one who would become a zealot. Before he closed the car door, Charlie told me his father was buried in Alabama and that he had never visited his grave. Could he do a story when Bobby returned to Reform after he was released? Not IF but WHEN he was released. I made the deal, and Charlie became one of Bobby's closest friends.

The public reaction to Bobby Joe's quest for 'Justice' was simply overwhelming. The *Globe Magazine* front cover showed Bobby sitting in a tee shirt with a ripped body, releasing a torrent of love letters that continued to flow into the office. Letters to the editor complained about the injustice. Hundreds of lawyers and court staff who filled our small downtown world, were a constant source of approval and congratulations.

We had more than a spring to our steps as we easily prepared our third Motion for a New Trial. We could recite the introductory language in our sleep. Mark Johnson's affidavit was the most important attachment. The Bromfield St. contingent was very confident, and very pleased when they received an early hearing date.

HABEAS CORPUS, AT LAST!

It was like old home week on October 8, 1986, on the eighth floor of the Suffolk County courthouse. Assistant District Attorney Fran O'Meara substituted for the retired John Kiernan. The two "Charlies," Kenney and Austin, arrived with a photographer and a cameraman.

Bob directed Mark Johnson's testimony, which was consistent with his statements to us. He introduced into evidence the map of the neighborhood and a weather report for September 27, 1970, to corroborate Johnson's testimony. He attached Kathleen Whiteside's trial testimony in which she described how she chased the assailants down the side street on the right-hand side off Talbot, Mallard Street.

I directed the testimony of "Rob" as he recalled how the inmate, who was most assuredly Peter Gardner, bragged about Bobby doing his time for murder.

It was a wonderful day, beautiful weather, and to top it off, I had tickets to the Red Sox who were playing a pennant playoff game at Fenway.

Judge Irwin granted a new trial on November 2, 1986. Now, after our third motion, we recognized the jurist for the brilliance, skill, acumen, and temperament he brought to this task. I was reminded of Mark Twain's view of his father when the author reached adulthood. He reportedly stated: "When I was fourteen, my father was so ignorant I could hardly stand to have him around. When I got to be twenty-one I was astonished at how much he had learned in seven years."

Bob and I immediately got a copy of the Irwin decision from the clerk's office. Danny Pokaski was the elected Clerk of the Suffolk Superior Court. I insisted Judge Irwin would want us to immediately bring Bobby to the courthouse. Danny signed and certified the Writ of Habeas Corpus to bring Bobby to court the next day to argue bail. It is the routine document the court issues to a correction center to transport an inmate to court. For us it was special: We finally got the Habeas we had been seeking since 1977!

We took the Writ ourselves to Bay State. Bobby was stunned, and we each hugged and tried without success to hide our joyful tears. This was the most important day in the rest of his life. When we walked away from Bay State Corrections, we knew it would be our last time there, and that Bobby would soon be saying a permanent goodbye to it.

We both squeezed into Big Bob's car. It was a white 2-seater 1979 911 Porsche. He took it as a fee from a former client. When it was delivered it was tangerine colored, had a sunburst rainbow in the rear window, a University of Berkeley logo, and California plates. It screamed *"The driver is a sinsemilla marijuana dealer."* He got pulled over too many times to count until he finally got a paint job.

As we approached interstate Route 95 Bob said out of the blue, "You know, I never really spent time climbing trees with you." I wanted to interrupt him before he became maudlin, thinking, "But, you were always a good dad," when he announced:

"You want to go a hundred miles an hour."

Then, whoosh, he hit the accelerator and the arrow pointed to the century mark on his speedometer, as we drove to the 1280 restaurant in Brookline for giddiness and drink with Charlie Kenney, my mother and brother Michael.

Bobby was released on his own recognizance the next afternoon. We threw a party at Governor's Alley, across from the Littlest Bar, that was like a dozen New Year celebrations. We called Bobby's father from the bar. I spoke to him, as he constantly repeated "Thank you…God bless you. I left him in the hands of the Good Master. Thank you."

DECEMBER 26, 1986: FREEDOM

In some quarters, December 26 is celebrated as *Boxing Day,* and is marked as a holiday when Christmas gift giving continues. Bobby Joe received the gift of freedom. It was not something that was given, so much as it was earned. The unalienable right to liberty, as declared by our colonial leaders for independence, is beyond government largess: it is endowed by the creator.

Still, the Suffolk County District Attorney had quite a say in whether Bobby's freedom would be forthcoming without a struggle, bearing in mind that the Judge Irwin decision simply ordered a new trial. The fact that it was nearly three months since Mark Johnson and others demonstrated the flaws of the first trial, irrefutably in our minds, created a growing sense of annoyance with the DA for not disclosing his intentions. That is, until Fran O'Meara gave us his progress report.

Fran, then and now, never doubted the weakness of the evidence against Bobby Joe. But before he would assent to a dismissal of the indictments, he was told by his boss, District Attorney Newman Flanagan, to answer one question: If not Bobby Joe, then who?

An interesting sidenote was that the *Boston Globe* was sorting out its pre-Christmas *Naughty and Nice* list. Charlie Kenney planned on naming Fran O'Meara as the top contender for the title, the Grinch that stole Christmas, for sitting on Bobby's case so long. We urged patience and short circuited that award.

Right after Judge Irwin issued his ruling, we made our entire file available to Fran. We briefed him on our investigation of Kelsey Reid and Peter Gardner's role in the Whiteside robbery and murder and shared our notes of statements from "Rob" and Mark Johnson. Our collaboration bore fruit.

In early December Fran notified us that he had spoken to a parolee who was living in California whom we had identified as being in the recreation room when the "new man" laughed about Bobby doing his time in front of "Rob." Using the circuitous method of allowing him to confirm the story, without being a snitch, Fran was satisfied that the "new man" was Peter Gardner.

A few weeks later Fran gave us the information we had been seeking since we identified the existence of the handgun taken from Kelsey Reid when he was arrested just two weeks after Levi Whiteside was killed. Fran told us he found the bullet that was taken from Levi Whiteside's body. For no explained reason, it was in a desk in the home study of the late Thomas Reardon, the trial prosecutor. Our *WTF* exclamation was shortened when he told us police ballisticians tested it and the slug matched up perfectly with the .22 caliber revolver thrown away by Kelsey Reid on October 14, 1970. This was our long overdue *hallelujah* moment.

Everything was in good order for our next and last court appearance. A week before Christmas I went to a hat store in South Boston to purchase a dozen black Scally caps, the *chapeau* of choice among Boston's ethnically Irish, and a close enough imitation of the Big Apple hat that Bobby Joe was wearing on the day of his arrest. I gave them as souvenir gifts to family and friends who supported Bobby's efforts. Several wore them on liberation day.

Even though the outcome was preordained, I had butterflies in my stomach as I entered the massive lobby of the Suffolk County courthouse. Bobby and his girlfriend June joined me as we took the elevator to the 7th floor. Bob and Ron were already there, as were Fran O'Meara and his police investigator. The presiding judge, Paul Chernoff was a welcome sight. I practiced in front of him dozens of times over the years, and he had the well-deserved reputation of the *Mensch on the Bench;* It's Yiddish for *a real good guy.* The case was called by Assistant Clerk Dana Leavitt. I was to become good friends with both when I was appointed to the Superior Court.

Fran addressed the Court, as it was the Commonwealth's Motion. He did not concede that Bobby Joe was innocent. In fact, he advised the court that Mrs. Whiteside and Nellie Rivera remained 100% convinced that Bobby was the shooter. I took no offense at this statement: Overly suggestive police arranged show ups create indelible memories of misidentifications. It is precisely for that reason that Bobby was snared in the vortex of his wrongful conviction. As Justice Brennan wrote in a landmark case, "It is a matter of common experience that, once a witness has picked out the accused at the lineup, he is not likely to go back on his word later on." Fran was reverse engineering our constitutional defense.

At long last, Fran summed up:

"District Attorney Flanagan believes that the interest of justice and public confidence in the courts requires at this time, that we can't say that Bobby Joe Leaster did it, and we can't say that he didn't, but he's served fifteen years. It's time to let go. The commonwealth moves to dismiss."

My future friend Judge Paul Chernoff dutifully intoned, "The Motion of the commonwealth is allowed with the assent of the defendant."

I was pleased that he was the one to endorse the order, while it was truly a pro forma exercise, brief, and to the point, because of Paul's reputation for integrity and compassion, it was a sweet coda to our ten-year quest for justice, and the conclusion of a sixteen-year nightmare for Bobby Joe.

There would be plenty of opportunities for conversations and applause for the remainder of the day. It is in their DNA for Muses to find reasons to celebrate.

I accepted the responsibility and that evening I hosted a party at my condo for at least a hundred people, including reporters from all the T.V. stations in Boston who televised our merriment live from my living room.

Few words of reflection were spoken; just smiles and giggles and crazy exuberance.

I stayed up through midnight with the last stragglers. Jim Byrne and Ted O'Brien helped me put my stereo in the window and I blasted Bob Dylan singing the ballad of Hurricane Carter through the North End streets:

This is the story of Hurricane
A man the authorities came to blame

For a crime he did not dooooooo

I think it was my neighbor Bob Carangelo who yelled to me to shut up.

"Good night Mr. Carangelo…. Merry Christmas, Mr. Carangelo," I replied

We smartly removed the stereo speakers and shut down the party.

I slept soundly and peacefully that night.

GOING HOME

A week after Christmas I received a delayed present. Billy Doherty had forwarded my "Progress Report" after our last SJC hearing to his friend Justice William Brennan, where I wrote that we relied on Brennan's important eyewitness decisions. Billy updated his friend with the news that justice was finally done. Billy gave me the return mail, where Justice Brennan wrote Bill: *"And my warmest best to Bob and Chris Muse. What an accomplishment. That's when lawyers are proudest of their profession."*

This was the highest praise I would ever earn. His praise was more compensation than I ever expected, and it was appreciatively received.

Other good things followed. The enormous press coverage of Bobby Joe's case from July through Christmas brought him his freedom and quite unexpectedly a train ride to Reform to visit his family, and a job on his return.

This feel-good story hit the national press and within days of Bobby's grant of a new trial, Big Bob received a $500.00 check from one of his Marine Squadron 323 buddies used to finance a round-trip Amtrak ticket to Alabama. When Charlie Kenny's article was printed, Scott Whetstone, a local contractor, contacted our office with the promise of a job as soon as Bobby Joe was released.

Charlie Austin accompanied Bobby Joe to Reform and his cameraman recorded the heart- breaking heart- warming moment when Bobby embraced his parents outside of their tiny sharecropper shack of a house.

William Hayes Leaster was a World War II veteran who instilled faith in God and hope in his son, and his 73-year-old suncreased face and quiet and thoughtful expressions of love told the story of a man who faced struggle after struggle throughout a poor and hard life, and who every day was a champion. His dad recorded again:

"I left him in the hands of the Good Master. I prayed for him every night. I got an answer today."

Leana Moore Leaster let her tears express the mother's faith that was contained in her heart until that moment of exquisite joy when she got that big hug Bobby had been saving for almost sixteen years. Bobby's 1000-watt smile said, *Mom, Dad, I'm home, and we'll be together forever.*

Bobby took a trip to Hopewell, his high school, which in 1972 was converted into an elementary school for all students. The previously all White Pickens County High School, on the top of a hill, now enrolled Blacks and Whites together. This side trip required a visit to the gym where Bobby had his happiest sporting moments. "Swish" and into the basket went the ball, as Bobby said, *I still have it.* In another moment he recounted how he could have gone to Jackson State on a basketball scholarship and said, *But instead I went to Boston, and that was a big mistake.*

He returned to Boston, to the South End, not far from the scene of his arrest. His girlfriend June and her son Andre provided immediate family and security to Bobby. In a few weeks he was working construction doing high end renovations with his new 'boss' and future lifelong friend, Scott Whetstone. After he read the *Globe Magazine* article, he simply *had* to offer Bobby a job. "I figured Bobby Joe needed a break." He hired a dedicated, and reliable worker, who was also quick to bond with his other employees.

I made friends with all these guys. I love making new friends. These guys here have such wonderful personalities and good attitudes. To be working around such nice fellows, it makes me feel warm inside. There is nothing out here that fazes me after what I went through for fifteen years in prison trying to keep my sanity. Being free feels good. It feels wonderful. It's like comin' back from the dead. Every day I wake up in the mornin' and I enjoy getting up. I know I can just walk out my door and go to work. I can't tell you how good that feeling is.

I am not bitter at all. I understand that a terrible, terrible mistake has been done to me. I understand that. And a lot of time has been taken out of my life for *nothin. I have said to myself over and over again, I'm not bitter, because at this point in my life, I have no time to be bitter. Because if I be bitter now and get out of here spending my time bein' bitter at the world, at the same time the world is passin' me by.*

The wedding party, under the watchful gaze of Abraham Lincoln, Hingham MA

Bobby continued to enjoy every morning he woke up to.
He and June welcomed their son into the world at Brigham and Women's hospital, and honoring his lawyers, named him Robert Joseph Christopher Leaster. In May 1988, Bobby was an usher at my wedding. Our families became forever united!

DISCHARGING A MORAL OBLIGATION

While Bobby quick-started his life of freedom, I kept my lawyer bulb shining bright in my head. Bobby deserved compensation for the years the state of Massachusetts stole from him.

I drew guidance from the Massachusetts constitution where John Adams wrote, *every subject of the commonwealth ought to find a certain remedy, by having recourse to the laws, for all injuries or wrongs.* I had the *wrong.* The search was on for the *remedy.*

Common Law tort principles offer a clear path for those injured to be compensated by those who caused the harm: When a car hits the pedestrian, file a claim against the driver; When a newspaper disparages a citizen, file a defamation claim;

Harassment? Assault? Medical malpractice? As they say, *Sue the Bastard!*

Bobby Joe's case was tricky. The judges had absolute immunity. The DA, absent corrupt motive was also protected. Police are often charged under civil rights statutes, but evidence of intentional deprivation of liberty is very difficult to find and present. In Bobby's case, we knew that Alton Frost's misstatement of the purpose for bringing Bobby Joe to City hospital to obtain the identification by Mrs. Whiteside, denied Bobby the opportunity to exclude corrupted evidence - the only evidence that connected him to the crime. However, the federal and state appeals courts undercut that argument by declaring, in so many words, that it did not make any difference, because it was still an accidental show-up when the police were transferring the suspect from one police jurisdiction to another. That excuse was tepidly offered at trial and could not withstand a commonsense examination. It was not like transferring spies at Checkpoint Charlie in Cold War Berlin. There was no policy or practice in effect in the police department's rules and regulations. Ordinarily, the wagon would have gone directly to District 3. That excuse was a pretext that anchored the admission of the suggestive and otherwise illegal identification.

Just as important, we did not want any more endless litigation. Bobby Joe had spent too much time with the courts already.

So, if we could not sue the City, what were we to do?

There were two cases in the prior decade of wrongfully convicted individuals who sought money from the Commonwealth. Lawyer Johnson and George Reissfelder had each filed a petition with the Massachusetts legislature seeking compensation from the state based on a theory of *Moral Obligation*. Each had been convicted of murder, and each had their conviction reversed. Neither was successful in obtaining payment from the State.

I obtained copies of their proposed legislation. I adapted the language to reflect Bobby Joe's case which asked that the state discharge a moral obligation for the wrongful conviction and the more than 15-year incarceration of an innocent man by awarding him compensation in the amount of $950,000.00. We had placed a value of $400.000.00 for the time we contributed to Bobby's cause. We made sure that all those who would review the legislation understood that we did not look for, nor would we accept, a penny.

My brother Michael was a well-regarded lobbyist for labor

unions and a few other clients, and he made all the introductions. One of four sponsors, all from Boston, was state representative Tom Finneran. A few words about him: He came from a traditional blue-collar neighborhood in Dorchester; he endorsed the return of the death penalty to the law of the Commonwealth; and he was something of a law-and-order guy. All that changed when he met Bobby.

"Fifteen years of a young man's life has just been taken away from him on the basis of a mistake made. It's a mistake that can happen to anyone at any time. When it does occur, we have an obligation to try to make up something. In our society remedy is typically financial. We certainly can't give him the 15 years he lost."

The legislation was filed, and a hearing was scheduled in late winter 1988. Bobby's testimony was powerful and well received. But like most legislative matters, it was all about the budget. Finneran predicted that opponents would claim it was not the right time. His response: "Well when the hell is the right time? It wasn't the right time to put this guy away for 15 years either, but we did it."

Tom's prediction was right on; the legislation died. But the right time was 1992, when Tom Finneran was the chairman of the Ways and Means Committee. One of the prerogatives of being chairman, was you could decide when the time was right.

In November 1992, Bobby was given a check for $75,000.00 as the first installment of a million-dollar annuity to be paid over twenty years. It was some cash to immediately help his father, as regrettably his mom had already passed away. The rest was to build a future. At a news conference he expressed appreciation but strongly told the many people listening to him in the State House hearing room that no amount of money could make up for his time in prison.

They took the best years out of my life. I want that understood.

The annuity and his weekly wages allowed Bobby to live a life beyond a level of the working poor. It also provided a thrust to address the equities of the other wrongfully convicted in Massachusetts. In 2004 a general law was passed which was modeled on the Leaster special law. Both laws identified the moral obligation to provide a remedy for the most egregious of wrongs.

Chapter Nine

TURNING OFF THE MACHINERY OF DEATH

Bobby Joe's case caused the politicians and the public to focus on their moral obligation to other matters, beyond the dollars in compensation for the wrongfully convicted. How would a person wrongfully sentenced to death for a crime he did not commit, get justice after his execution? It was not an empty thought, as it is a question posed almost automatically when one more execution is scheduled, and the pleas to governors for clemency are publicized, as vigils sprout up outside the prison walls. When there is a surge of crime, especially police killings and the heinous murders of the most innocent victims, the historic response has been the cry to bring back the electric chair. That cry was heard often in Massachusetts, and frequently after Bobby's release. And his case provided guidance during those cries and responses.

Bobby Joe still recoils when he remembers the moment the jury returned its verdict. They were instructed that if they, the Jury, found Bobby Joe Leaster guilty of murder in the first degree, they must then consider whether he should be electrocuted. Whenever Bobby speaks about hearing the jury's verdict, he gets emotional, and his memory of his fright is palpable.

I was expecting the jury to say we find Bobby Joe innocent and I would go home. When the judge asked the jury, do you sentence Bobby Joe to death, my knees buckled.

In 1971 Massachusetts like most states had a death penalty on its books. The last time Old Sparky lit up Charlestown Prison was in 1947 when two murderers of a U. S. Marine were executed. While Massachusetts courts showed some reluctance to impose the death penalty, it is the state that hung a dozen witches in Salem and, over world-wide protest, sent Sacco and Vanzetti to their deaths.

In 1972, in *Furman v. Georgia,* the Supreme Court voided all death penalty sentences in the 40 states that had such laws and ordered a stay of all executions. It wrote that the discretion of judges and juries in imposing the death penalty was too often arbitrary and inconsistent and, as one concurring justice noted, "It is the poor, the sick, the ignorant, the powerless and the hated who are executed."

In the aftermath of Furman, states enacted laws presumed to follow the prohibitions of Furman. Massachusetts passed such a law in 1982 that was later struck down by the Supreme Judicial Court. In every election, statewide and local, the hot button issue was debated during campaigns and in almost every legislative session, a bill reinstating the death penalty was proposed. In each instance the opponents brought forward the wrongful conviction of Bobby Joe.

The issue sparked a debate between candidates looking to succeed Mayor Flynn. The Suffolk County Sheriff, Bob Rufo, challenged the Police Commissioner's support for a death penalty citing studies showing disproportionate impact on minorities, its failure to deter crime, and cost, and because:

"The system is fraught with human error. If Massachusetts had the death penalty [Commissioner] Roache has proposed, Bobby Joe Leaster could be dead today."

During one packed legislative hearing in July 1994, Governor Bill Weld urged passage of a pending bill. His Lieutenant Governor had candidly acknowledged that it was possible innocent persons could be executed, but that "it was an acceptable price to pay" in order to have that punishment. Joe McIntyre, the chairman of the committee, requested Bobby Joe to come forward, and asked the Governor "to look this man in the eye and tell him why making a mistake that would sacrifice his life would be an acceptable price to pay." The bill did not get out of committee.

Supreme Court Justice Harry Blackmun, who had earlier approved standards for a "constitutional" death penalty statute, reversed himself in 1994, writing:

"It is virtually self-evident to me now that no combination of procedural rules or substantive regulations ever can save the death penalty from its inherent constitutional deficiencies." He therefore announced, "from this day forward, *I no longer shall tinker with the machinery of death.*"

But the tinkering continued. The Governor, one more time, pushed for a death penalty. Tom Finneran a staunch opponent, and recently elected Speaker of the House of Representatives announced that the 1996 proposal would not get legislative approval. He explained his opposition:

"Three little words; *Bobby Joe Leaster.*"

Everything seemed to change in the fall of 1997. Ten-year-old Jeffrey Curley was kidnapped from his neighborhood in Cambridge. Two men, pedophiles, sexually assaulted the 80-pound Jeffrey, then suffocated him. The next day they drove his body to Maine, where they placed him in a 50-gallon plastic container, filled it up with cement, and tossed the child into a river in South Berwick. The two suspects were arrested within days, and subsequently convicted of kidnaping and murder.

The public outrage was spontaneous. All murders are horrible. But with Jeffrey, an innocent child lured away by the promise of a bicycle, abducted in a safe neighborhood, sexually assaulted by grown men, and his body disposed like trash-this was horrific, unspeakable. If ever there was a case that cried out for the ultimate penalty, it was this.

Within days, a previously filed death penalty bill was resurrected and within a month of Jeffrey's abduction, was scheduled for a vote. The Senate already voted in favor of it. The Governor was ready to sign it into law. The House was nearly evenly divided, and the vote was too close to predict.

As expected, the public discussion was heated and divisive, with hardened opinions. The *Boston Globe* reached out to Bobby for his comments:

"I'm a living example of what could happen." He stressed his religious beliefs saying, *"Only God can take a life. I understand what they [the family] are going through but voting for the death penalty is not rational at all."*

His words were not effective enough, at least in the short term. A few days after the interview the House of Representatives passed the Death Penalty Bill by a single vote.

John Slattery represented the North Shore city of Peabody and voted in favor of the bill. Coincidentally, Chief Justice Liacos was a resident of Peabody. He had told others that his Single Justice decision ordering a new trial for Bobby was among the top three most important in his judicial career. A few years earlier Bobby Joe and I began a 25-year annual presentation to a group of high school kids who interned during the summer in different court departments. He became the favorite of each class of the Judicial Youth Corp. In 1995 Chief Justice Liacos attended the first session in the SJC chamber. He walked up to Bobby, touched him affectionately on the shoulder, apologized to him for what had happened, and told the kids that Bobby Joe "teaches you courage, hope, persistence and self-esteem."

Paul Liacos scheduled a meeting with his representative, not as the Chief Justice, but as a constituent. He discussed the Bobby Joe case and urged John Slattery to reconsider his vote, which he did, courageously, the next legislative day, killing the legislation, but subjecting himself to the wrath of death penalty advocates, and political opposition in future elections. Slattery, many years later noted that he had educated himself on the discriminatory application of the death penalty nationwide, targeting the poor and minorities, and how it resulted in the deaths of innocent people. He cited Bobby Joe as the best-known example of that. His first vote, he noted seventeen years after it, was based on the prevailing opinion of his constituents when he believed his votes should reflect their position. He changed his vote because he discovered that "sound- thinking elected officials owe their constituents their best judgement." Massachusetts continues to remain free of a death penalty.

Yet, the drumbeat for executions continues as the ultimate moral issue of our time.

One example that shows a stress point between morality and *The Law,* can be found in the 2019 Supreme Court decision, *Madison v. Alabama*, where the court postponed the execution of the defendant who was convicted thirty years earlier of murdering a police officer. He had suffered a series of strokes and now suffered from vascular dementia. He demonstrated an inability to recall the crime he had committed, and arguably had a "mental state [that] is so distorted by a mental illness" that he lacks an understanding of "the State's rationale for his execution." The eighth amendment prohibition for cruel and unusual punishment would foreclose his execution. The case was remanded to the lower court for further review.

This is how the minority opinion began:

What the Court has done in this case makes a mockery of our Rules. …. Petitioner's counsel convinced the Court to stay his client's execution and to grant his petition for a writ of certiorari for the purpose of deciding a clear-cut constitutional question…he switched to an entirely different argument [at the hearing].

In other words, the defendant should be executed because his lawyer committed a pleading error.

Within weeks of the 1916 Easter Rising, the Catholic rebellion in Dublin that ignited a successful separation from the British, more than a dozen of its leaders were arrested, held in the dungeons of the nearby Kilmainham Gaol, tried, convicted, and executed by firing squads. James Connolly, severely wounded during the insurrection, was a day or two away from death, when he was taken from an infirmary on a stretcher, bound to a chair, in front of the dreary gray stone walls of the prison yard, and shot by British soldiers. More than any other execution, Connolly's galvanized world outrage, that turned public opinion against the excesses of the Empire.

It is a sad commentary that some judges have become so desensitized to the most important decisions they could make from the bench, that their first concern was whether a lawyer was playing around with court procedures. Executing those with mental challenges, dementia, and other disabilities is right up there with strapping a person on the brink of death to a chair so the executioners had a non-moving target.

Studies have shown that the death penalty is not a deterrent to murder. Experts have statistically analyzed cases that continue to demonstrate the disparate treatment of the minorities and the poor. And, of course, whether God would approve of legislating death is a question that must be reserved to Judgment Day. But the one incontrovertible argument is that innocent people have been executed. There is no reason to look further than Bobby Joe Leaster.

Radha Natarajan, executive director of the New England Innocence Project, can rattle off those statistics as easily as a Patriots fan can cite the number of Super Bowl wins quarterbacked by Tom Brady. The numbers are staggering. The recent arrival of DNA among investigative tools, a blood type and human fluid matching test, provides a statistical certainty of innocence (or guilt) greater than a billion to one. With DNA, hundreds of the wrongfully convicted have been exonerated. More than 70% of them were convicted based on faulty eyewitness identification.

One reason we were always swimming upstream, against strong currents, during every one of our appeals, was the doctrine of *Finality of Conviction*. It is premised on a view that once a defendant has been convicted and sentenced, and all appeals have concluded, the government has a strong interest in preserving that final judgement. Many reasons have been cited, but the three most common ones are the costs of re-litigation, the difficulties with new trials using old evidence, and the loss of confidence in the judicial system.

Naturally, the Muse team took a more expansive position, and it was best laid out in the earlier hearing with Judge Irwin when we responded to his inquiry, how long will this appeal continue, and I stated, "Until Justice is done." Judges and Justices had a stubborn allegiance to a doctrine that invited violations of Due Process of law. Our possibly cynical view was that problems of administrative efficiency drove the policy in Massachusetts.

The constitutional right of Habeas Corpus, the procedural right that Bobby Joe exercised three times before we entered our appearances, was dramatically limited in the years following our federal appeal. Bobby and I were invited by Professor Charles Ogletree to participate in a Harvard Law School forum on *The future of Habeas Corpus*. One participant was the New Jersey federal judge who freed Ruben "Hurricane" Carter. He responded to the now growing concern that prisoner claims were clogging the courts with his recollection that during the year he heard Carter's "Habe" appeal, he spent eight weeks on a Medicaid fraud civil case that was settled mid-trial, and asked, "What was the greater waste of judicial resources?"

In 1990 the Supreme Court drew a line in the sand that I could not wrap my head around. It dismissed the petition of a Texas death row inmate, holding that a claim of actual innocence based on newly discovered evidence does not state a ground for habeas corpus relief. My youth and inexperience did not prevent me from declaring the absurdity of that proposition. Bobby Joe said it more eloquently when he rebuked the reasoning of our SJC Justices who denied him his final appeal five years earlier: *"How did I get a fair trial if I am innocent?"*

In 1996, Congress passed legislation that curbed the number of post-conviction appeals by death row inmates with the *Antiterrorism and Effective Death Penalty Act*. The Act imposes limits on how often and under what circumstances prisoners in state or federal custody may petition for federal habeas relief. The purpose of the law, motivated by political concerns about appearing soft on crime, was transparent in its words, *Effective Death Penalty Act*, and the title sickened me as much as the restraints it placed on access to justice.

This doctrine of *Finality of Conviction* was the judicial climate that chilled our efforts on behalf of an objectively innocent man. It remains a policy that is a headwind stalling other innocent men and women from getting their justice.

Bobby Joe with fellow exonerees at 2019 New England Innocence Project Reception.

MIRACLE WORKER

One evening in the winter of 1991, I took Bobby Joe to Michael's Waterfront restaurant in the North End. It was traditional for us to go for beers and burgers after speaking engagements. We had just spoken at Boston College Law School, as we would for almost the next thirty years. The students had the jaw dropping experience of hearing and seeing real life criminal justice. Bobby returned to my B C Law Trial Practice class every year, causing at least a few of those students to write in their evaluations that it was the best single class in law school.

We ran into Bobby Wheeler at the bar. Bobby was on our law school team and drafted most of our First Circuit appeal brief, and was now a well-respected criminal defense lawyer. He had not seen Bobby since his Christmas gift of freedom, and the former student-lawyer and his client had much to catch up on. In a short while the conversation shifted to the name game, as in, "I represented a guy in Norfolk, did you know him?" The two 'Bobbys' went back and forth. Bobby W. mentioned a major drug dealer, and Bobby L. knew when he was committed. Bobby W. mentioned a major mafia boss. Bobby replied, " *He saw me in the South End when I was just released. He pulled over in his big Cadillac and yells 'Hey Bobby. Congratulations' and he give me a hundred-dollar bill."*

Michael's had a roast beef carving station where for a dollar you could get a thick sandwich. The idea was to feed the customers, so they stayed to keep buying drinks: It worked. Bobby went to get one. About a half hour later I noticed he had disappeared for a long time. When he returned, I asked him if he got lost?

No, he told me *I ran into a friend, Jose, who was making the sandwiches.*

I always saw Bobby as a client, then as a friend. I never focused on his time in prison. The conversations that night reminded me that he was also an *Ex-Con*, not in a pejorative way, of course, but as one who knew life in prison and its occupants. Jose was one of them.

Boston like every major city was dealing with spiraling drug and gang crimes. A detective detailed to the DEA, Drug Enforcement Agency, joined me for coffee one morning and told me he had just left a meeting: They were learning about this new drug, Crack Cocaine, that was sweeping east from California. "They make crystals out of coke, and then you smoke it. It's almost instantly addictive. It's cheap. Street gangs are selling it like they had franchises with McDonalds. And, you know, you don't put two McD's next to each other. These guys fight off competition. It's ugly. It's coming our way."

It came too soon.

In August 1988 Tiffany Moore, a twelve-year-old girl, was sitting on a mailbox near her Humboldt Ave. Roxbury home, when she got caught in the crossfire of rival drug dealers and died from two stray bullets. Her death brought emotional paralysis to the city, and outrage from her community. This was not bad guys shooting bad guys: Tiffany could have been anyone's daughter. It was a sickening moment in time. That, the sudden explosion of drug and gang activity and the historic spike in youth homicides, caused me to look at Bobby differently.

"Bobby. What do you think is happening with these kids and gangs and guns and shootings"?

"Chris a lot of them are just babies. They don't know better. They are lost and the gangs give them family."

"You know Bobby, you're the kind of guy they would listen to. I hate to remind you, but you are an ex-con. Did you ever think about working with them, to straighten them out?"

"If I could save just one young man from dying or going to jail, it would be worth it."

I had recently received an offer from a major contractor to put Bobby to work. It was not yet finalized, and I reminded Bobby that a union construction job was still on the table and that it and overtime would put a lot of money in his pocket. Bobby did not hesitate; working with kids would be more valuable.

I got on it the next day. I called Channel 4's Charlie Austin who had developed a wonderful friendship with Bobby. Bobby often travelled to his Lexington home to hang out with his family and sometimes fish with Charlie at a nearby river. I told him my plan to get Bobby working with troubled Boston kids. Did he have any ideas?

"I'm going to the Martin Luther King breakfast next Monday and I'll be sitting next to Mayor Flynn at the head table for three hours. He'll hear a lot about Bobby."

A few days later, Charlie happily reported "The Mayor was interested."

Now, I knew that there could be a lot of light between "being interested" and giving someone a job. So, my next call was to my friend Mike Taylor who had a high-level position with the City. I told him that the Mayor was "interested" in helping Bobby and asked him to search out possibilities. Within a month, Mike called with news that the city was setting up a new program to work with the most difficult kids in Boston and Bobby would be among the next appointments.

Robert Lewis, a youth worker employed at the Boston Community Centers, was directed by Mayor Ray Flynn to do something to intervene with the gang members, to "interrupt the violence." The Mayor's decision to give Robert a blank canvas- the paints and brushes would come later- was fortuitous. It was the start of the Street Worker Program.

"It was me, Tracy, Chops and Bill Paulson a star football player from Southie. I started it with a plan drawn on one sheet of paper. I went out and bought these big blue jackets with a sun on the back. It lit up at night. If a cop saw it, he knew we were on the street."

Robert was raised in East Boston in the Maverick Street Housing Projects with his mother and five siblings. After the McKay Middle School, he headed to East Boston High where he was welcomed into a place where, except for the prevailing Italian American ethnicity, it could have been a setting from the TV series, *Happy Days*, or for real television archivists, *Welcome Back Kotter*. Sports were dominant, athletes were kings, cheerleaders were starlets, football games were filled to capacity, proms were spectacular, and running for student office was raucous. Robert was a three-sport star, class officer and one of the most popular in the class. He was happiest there, and remains in contact with other alumni, especially his teammates and his coaches.

I remember him as one of the few Black students in Eastie, Robert remembers me as looking a bit different from other teachers: "I can still see you with that long hair hanging over your collar."

It was true: I cannot say that I blended easily at East Boston H.S. My first day was memorable as I harkened to the sage advice of Carmen Scarpa, headmaster and football coach, who provided succinct, direct, and clear new-man training:

"Mr. Muse, you look like you stepped out of a band box, nice suit, nice tie, but when you get down to your feet, well there's a problem. Those shoes you wear (Boat Shoes) and no socks, well these kids won't understand this. They expect you to wear real shoes, and unless you have no money, you should have socks. If money is an issue, well, I will help out."

I see Carmen from time to time and his first action is to tug up my cuffs to see if I am wearing socks.

Junior, as he was known, excelled in all sports and was a welcome fixture in the projects. His was one of fewer than two dozen Black families. Even though accepted by everyone in his almost all White neighborhood, or so he thought, he dated White girls very much on the sly and in the shadows. His friends were tough, and back in the day, organized crime, the Italian kind, had a presence in Eastie. Many of his friends carried guns. However as one student told me: "But, Mr. Muse, we'd never take them to school, and we always put them away when we went to our clubs." Junior recalls that he spoke with ease with terms like "goombah" and "fuhgeddaboudit," and knew to refer to spaghetti "gravy," not sauce, as any good Italian boy would.

Everything was perfect until his best friend firebombed his apartment when he was sixteen years old.

One practical decision made by the federal judge was to delay by a year the busing of students into East Boston, and then limiting it to bringing in minority students and not busing residents out. I was teaching there that year and, as the other parts of the city exploded in protest and violence, East Boston was subdued, as the inevitable integration of its high school was pursued with careful planning.

Originally known as Noddle Island, East Boston is separated from the rest of the city by a harbor, and reachable only by a tunnel, the one from downtown that continues to Logan Airport. Although the court and the busing managers reported that this special treatment was because of the geographic isolation of Eastie and the transportation difficulty, everyone in Eastie thought otherwise: the establishment was afraid Eastie would shut down the tunnel by everything from massive picketing at the opening of the tunnel, to flat tires at rush hour, to bombs. And, if they shut down Callahan Tunnel, they would destroy airport commerce as well.

Busing Blacks into East Boston ripped open the racial prejudice that simmered below the surface. Now, Eastie was part of the city-wide busing plan, and racist lunacy took hold. In May 1976, Junior's sophomore year, after one school year of busing, tribal hate took over and Blacks were not welcomed to live among them. Some of the teenagers thought that being White carried with it a loyalty test; you were either with the Whites and against the Blacks, or you were an outcast. The best thing that Junior can say about his best friend, the one he played sports with and whose mother often gave him dinner, was that, when he threw the Molotov cocktail into his courtyard one of the older boys put it in his hand and asked, "Are you one of us or one of them." It did not cut it as an excuse, nor did it garner forgiveness.

Junior and his family moved to a housing complex in the South End, where, he says with humor and irony, "I had to forget

Italian slang and learn more Black street jargon." His continuing resentment went towards his friends and neighbors who did not reach out with support, the ones who stood by silently as twenty Black families were socially evicted. At that time, the Boston Housing Authority oversaw *de facto* segregated, race-based tenant selection. It remained so until the end of the next decade when Mayor Ray Flynn agreed to a city-wide desegregation plan under a federal court consent decree.

But, while Junior was uprooted from his home, he refused to give up his school. He already was enrolled in Eastie, so he would not become one of those statistics, one who was bussed to it. He declined a seat on a bus for transportation to his high school, instead taking the Orange, then the Blue Line to Maverick station, and then onward to his beloved East Boston High School where more honors awaited a prize running back and future U-Mass standout, and civic leader.

When Junior started the Street Worker program, he had experienced the worst and the best of Boston. Tracy, Chops, Paul, and Junior started walking the streets. They went right up to the guys on the corner like the "X-Men" the 'GOYAs, Mozart Park, and his own Villa Victoria., to "interrupt" gang violence. They communicated with beepers, and used numbers to identify themselves, numbers to identify locations, and numbers like the universal call for assistance, 911. Tracy, or perhaps all of the squad identified Junior with the number "666", the ancient designation for the devil. The devil and his Street Worker disciples became impact players. They made inroads with the gangs and earned trust from their leaders.

When the Vamp Hill gang shot up the Morning Star Baptist Church, the Black ministers from the Roxbury-Mattapan-Dorchester triangle issued their call to action. They organized a meeting of civic leaders and church representatives from across the city. Junior went to the meeting location that evening but was denied admittance because he was not on the list of invitees. One of the ministers saw him standing outside and declared that if Junior did not get in, he would not enter as well. Twenty minutes later Junior lead the Reverends; Eugene Rivers, Bruce Wall, Jeffrey Brown, and Ray Hammond, on a street tour. He brought them to the Academy Homes project and Junior introduced the men of the cloth to members of the Timberwolves. Like Humphrey Bogart said in the movie, "It was the beginning of a beautiful friendship."

There were a dozen major gangs in the city, and Mayor Ray Flynn gave Junior open-ended support. This included more Street Workers and more blue jackets. One of the next to wear one was Bobby Joe.

"I remember interviewing Bobby. I knew his whole story. Everyone did. I remember how he had no bitterness, how he wanted to help kids. After 45 minutes I hired him." Because of municipal funding procedures, Bobby's position would not start until the beginning of the next fiscal year, July 1. But Robert, the head of the program, insisted they would put Bobby Joe to work sooner.

He found money to pay Bobby a "stipend" of $250 a week so that Bobby could go to high schools to speak to the students about his case. I had done this with Bobby in Boston and neighboring towns at every level of school, college, and law school, and knew that he would hit home runs with the kids. He was inspirational and motivated the students. It was also a good opportunity for Bobby to connect to his new responsibilities as a Street Worker.

Bobby filled the auditoriums at every district high school – Dorchester, East Boston, Charlestown, South Boston, Madison, English, West Roxbury, Hyde Park—every section of the city.

Afterwards, the young people would come up and talk to me. So, when I went out on the streets, they recognized me. When I left the high schools, I shadowed the street workers. I teamed up

with George Porter, who we called Chops, after July 1, 1991, when I went full time, and he showed me the ropes. He took me to Bromley Heath Projects. I went to an apartment of a lady, Mildred Hailey who was kind of in charge of the tenants. Chops was very nice. "This is Bobby Joe. He'll be working with me. He was wrongly convicted of murder. I'm telling him what's going on here in the project. He's here to help."

The Bromley-Heath housing project was built in the early 40's in an area between Jamaica Plain and Roxbury, that became a no man's land. The thousand apartments in low and high-rise buildings were isolated, disconnected from the rest of the city, and became a high crime zone. The facilities went into decay and disrepair as the Boston Housing Authority lost its ability to manage the property. In the early 70's long time tenant Mildred Hailey had enough and spearheaded the formation of the Bromley- Heath Tenant Management Corp. She and the corporation took over the day-to-day management of the physical plant and also directed efforts at the addiction, jobless, youth and crime problems within the 23-acre mini city. After Mildred died in 2015 Mayor Marty Walsh renamed Bromley Heath after her. This was the Mildred Hailey who Chops introduced Bobby Joe to.

Chops passed away in 2010. We had become good friends. He was tall, over 6 feet five, and large. He brought me around to the gang members. They'd see him and say, " Hey, Uncle Chops, what's up." They'd give him some love. You could see they respected him. He'd tell them about me. They always heard about my situation. He'd tell them I was working with him; they'd see me in the project. Chops gave me insight on what was going on. Gang members did not like outsiders. Chops was accepted. He took me to all the courthouses and introduced me. The judges knew me, the chief probation officers like Bernie Fitzgerald in Dorchester knew me. Court officers would wave me through without the searches and metal detectors. They still do. I'd stand up for the kids that were caught for minor things like shoplifting. Never guns or serious things. I got their trust by helping them.

Bobby's first assignment after signing on full time was working directly in one of the most troubled high schools, the Jeramiah E. Burke, the "Jerry" as it was widely known.

I went to the Burke just like the teachers. We started at 8:30 in the morning and went to 2:30. We kept the halls clear, told the kids to take off their hat, stop hanging in the bathrooms and things like that. We made sure they didn't smoke weed. In the halls going to other classes, they'd get into arguments. I broke them up. I did a lot of talking to them. Sometimes just chilling. Sometimes serious stuff about school and home. I got along good with them. After school, I stayed around the neighborhood. Did the same thing. Just being around, getting to know them. It worked. I got respect from them.

Robin Christian joined the street worker program soon after Bobby. She is home grown, raised in Boston her entire life except for college. After graduating from Jamaica Plain High School in 1985 she attended the University of Iowa on a basketball scholarship. What she will not tell you is that she was first team High School All American. Her coach Jerry Howland will proudly fill in those blanks. Jerry became very much part of Bobby Joe's life and his story.

When Robin graduated, she returned to her Humboldt Ave. Roxbury home and began work at the Shelbourne Community Center. For a year and a half, her situation was near perfect as she gave back to the community. Then one day, near her home at the intersection of Crawford Street, her life changed.

"I heard shots, three or four of them. I ran to Crawford Street to see what happened. I saw a kid lying on the street, not moving. I got close. I saw grey matter coming out of his head. I knew this young man as "Black." I still don't know his birth name. I knew then I had to do something to change this insanity, this violence. I signed up with the Street Workers."

Robin joined Bobby at the "Jerry", her first assignment:

"He was good, really good. I called him "the Regulator." He made sure the kids all followed the regulations, to move along in the hallways, to get to class, not to fight. When you talk to him as a friend, he has to raise his voice. He was LOUD with the kids; you could hear him down the hall. But he was the Gentle Giant. Once he got your attention, you know a fresh kid that calls him an asshole, or something, he can go from a stern voice to a soft one, after he gets their cooperation. He was like that on the streets too."

Bobby's new career soon evolved into working directly with the burgeoning gang population and involved one-on-one intervention on the streets during "business hours," that is usually late afternoon into the evening. It included everything from getting summer jobs, arranging for jobs and housing transition for some held in the house of correction, and sometimes just talking. When they learned that one gang was going to retaliate against another, Bobby was there with his coworkers to talk peace. He stood with Mayor Flynn and Police Commissioner Mickey Roache when they canvassed the neighborhoods in the wake of the acquittal of Rodney King's police assailants at a time when riots erupted in LA and beyond.

The worst part of Bobby Joe's job was the funerals– for those who were innocent victims caught in the crossfire or for those who died shooting at other rival gang members. Over thirty years he attended 800 funerals, sometime to grieve for ones he knew, and sometimes to provide security during burial ceremonies when gang rivals showed up.

Blue Hill Avenue was laid out more than a century and a half ago as a boulevard from the edge of Boston's Roxbury district, through the fringes of Dorchester, heading west as a state road to the little bit of 'Vermont' ten miles from downtown, known as the Blue Hills Reservation. There is a ski slope, hiking trails and horse stables. It is a couple of miles and a world apart from the Mattapan section that marks the end of the Avenue, and from a prominent African-American religious gathering center,The Morning Star Baptist Church.

In May 1992, there was yet another funeral for a young man who was killed in a drive- by shooting. At least a dozen rival gang members stormed the church and went on a stabbing and shooting spree, leaving several seriously injured, mourners in a state of shock, and a city outraged.

In its aftermath, clergy and civic and political leaders coalesced to dive headlong into identifying causes and seeking solutions for Black and Latino youth violence. The plan that evolved was to ignite a better relationship with the police, and to join forces with community agencies and probation services and to directly intervene with the gang members and other at-risk youth. *Operation Ceasefire*, as it became known, caused a two-thirds reduction in homicides and a commensurate reduction in assaults and gun possessions. In its first 27 months there was not one homicide of a youth 17 years old or younger. The early success was heralded as the *Boston Miracle*. Street Workers were on the front lines. Bobby

Joe Leaster was among the miracle workers.

CHRIS BYNER

Chirs became another lifer with the Street Workers beginning in 1995 and continuing to this day. He is homegrown, raised
in the very tough Orchard Park Housing Project in Roxbury, the
second youngest of 14 siblings. He attended the John McCormack
Middle School in Dorchester. It backs up to the BC High campus
and was fenced off literally and figuratively when I was a student
there. The closest we came to the mostly Black seventh and eighth
graders was when we saw them at play near the fence separating
our parking lot where we were allowed to smoke. That changed
when Chris was at the McCormack. He was an early star at basketball and track and also a high honors student. BC High had developed a relationship with its neighbor and a teacher at the McCormack recognized talent and promise in Chris: He arranged for a
scholarship to my high school alma mater. Chris lasted a year before he acknowledged that he missed girls and transferred a mile
away to South Boston High.

"My brothers went to Southie at the start of busing. It was
different when I got there but there were remnants of the troubles.
The buses bringing us from Roxbury drove in caravans until my
senior year. And most of us never went to stores or into the community. I did though. I didn't care. I was an honor student and did
really well on the track team and with basketball. I stayed late for
practice and went to my friends' homes sometimes. The school
was 50-50 Black-White, and I had White friends. I spent a lot of
time in the D Street projects."

We got a lot of business from the D Street projects when I
worked that summer in the South Boston District Court. It was low
income, mostly welfare, and tough. We arraigned several murders
where bodies were left in a hallway or a dumpster near the projects.
Alcoholism was rampant. Violence was routine. Somehow families survived, and many of the kids escaped, usually with the help
of an interested adult or mentor. One of them was Billy, a hockey
star at Southie and a friend of Chris.

"One time I went to Billy's apartment in the projects after
school, and Billy went to the bathroom. His 8-year-old brother
saw me all alone and said, 'Who let the nigger in here?'

Laughing, Billy got all upset and I told him, " It's no re-flection on you. It's what he learned. Adults were talking, not kids. Compared to college, I had more in common with kids in Southie than anywhere. We were literally the same only different color."

Chris received a full scholarship to Brandeis University in suburban Waltham in 1985, based on grades and basketball. It was a different environment, not as diverse as now, but welcoming. He majored in American Studies and Sociology.

When Chris Byner left the Orchard Park Housing project for the Brandeis campus, Darryl Whiting from Queens, New York moved in. He set up an elaborate drug processing and distribution center there with some associates from Queens. They became known as the New York Boys. Whiting became known as "God."

"God" and his "Boys" effectively owned Orchard Park. They took control of multiple apartments where they diluted and packaged up to five kilograms of cocaine a week, imported from New York City, for sale as powder and as crack. Whiting estab-lished elaborate security, communicating by walkie- talkie to more than 100 'employees' who delivered the drugs to other parts of Or-chard Park for another level of distribution, or sale on the streets. His trusted associates from the Queens provided enforcement that often included murder for such capital offenses as holding back money or 'disrespecting' the senior operatives or their girlfriends. It was a 24 hour a day operation, and at its peak, would generate $200,000 a day.

Couriers took weekly flights to NYC to purchase kilos of cocaine. One immunized courier told the federal grand jury that she would take the Eastern Shuttle to LaGuardia with a money belt with thousands of dollars. On arrival she would taxi less than a mile to a bar in Queens and exchange the cash for two or more kilos of powder. In the bathroom, she would strap the cocaine un-der her dress, "As you can see, I am a large size woman. My pack-ages didn't even show a bulge under my dress," then, a shuttle back to Boston.

With the millions of dollars spilling into the new economy, "God" Whiting bought local businesses in Roxbury including bar-ber shops video stores and real estate. "God" also sprinkled the money in the community with barbecues, concerts, and handouts of money. Some of the teenage runners made a thousand dollars a week.

In December 1990, a wide-ranging federal investigation led to the indictment of more than fifty members of the organization, the disbandment of the New York Boys, and the lifetime imprisonment of "God". It did not end drug sales and gang violence in Orchard Park, not by a long shot.

Chris returned home after graduation in 1989, to a neighborhood that had changed for the worse, when he first noticed the proliferation of gangs. His Brandeis degree opened many doors, including one at a downtown investment company. His banker's salary allowed Chris to move to my neighborhood, the North End, renting a small apartment on Salem Street near the Old North Church. His first-floor neighbor was an older Italian woman who constantly fed him. He fondly recalls the homemade sausage and meatballs, and smiles. He grimaces when he talks about his workplace:

"There were bad things happening at my home neighborhood that really got to me. There was crack, gangs, guns, and HIV Aids. The shootings were in the news every day. It's all I saw on TV. It really concerned me. But it meant nothing to people at work. Every day at the water bubbler or at lunch, no one talked about it. All my co-workers talked about was the market, money, or a party they went to. I was troubled by it every day that it was not part of their discussion. I needed something more. So I quit. I ran out of money in a few months, so I left and moved back in with my mom."

Employment did not jump out at the recycled *Yuppie*, no longer wearing pricey suits to a downtown job or inhabiting a gentrified section of Boston. He took a home health aide position in The North Community Center, a satellite clinic operated by the Roxbury Comprehensive located in the middle of Orchard Park. After training, he worked with patients who needed encouragement to visit the clinic for care, also prompting them to take their medicine and return to their appointments. He administered blood sticks to monitor diabetes. He distributed condoms to battle the Aids epidemic He took blood pressure and seemed to always wear a stethoscope outside his shirt or jacket.

During his walks through the housing project, he noticed something unsettling: Each of the dozens of buildings surrounded open area courtyards which, since he was a kid, were always gathering spots and play areas for kids and young teenagers: Now, they were eerily quiet. Gangs and drugs were everywhere. Gun shots could be heard regularly. Mothers would no longer allow their kids outside to play. It was an echo to Rachel Carson's *Silent Spring*, when another kind of chemical silenced birds, bees, and other wildlife. Chris was reminded again that something had to be done.

During those same walks Chris befriended the gang bangers, the drug dealers, and the drug users. They saw him as a "poor" rock star because he grew up in OC and went to college, and also because he gave them condoms. They called him 'doctor' because of his stethoscope. Chris was skilled at talking without judging them. He wanted them to have safe sex, come to the health center, and most importantly, not die. He allowed them to see the wisdom of his suggestions, and eventually he started a youth education program at the clinic. This initial success led to a full-time job as a youth worker at the community center. Within a year, two Street Workers working with the Orchard Park gang noticed Chris Byner and his successes. Bobby Joe and Tracy encouraged Chris to join them. The rest, as they *sort of* say, was his future.

Before Chris received his first City of Boston paycheck, Bobby Joe had already left his mark on most of the gangs in Boston, including Orchard Park in Roxbury, the MS 13 in East Boston and all of the namesakes of streets in Mattapan and Dorchester, like Castlegate, Intervale, and Magnolia, and those gangs that associated with professional sports teams like the Steelers. As Chris recounts:

"He'd go anywhere. I remember when he went to East Boston and worked with the gangs that spoke Spanish, and him with just English. But he connected: He could engage like no one else. He was oblivious to danger. He had a way with guys on the corner. He's a chameleon, he just transforms himself wherever he goes. A lot of folks intrude on territory. He allows them to bring him in."

Bobby Joe explained his lack of fear:

They all knew my situation. They knew I did 15 1/2 years for a crime I did not commit. They saw I wasn't afraid to talk to them, and the gang members respected that. I still had the prison mentality. Inside, I had to be on guard 24 hours a day. I had no fear. These were just kids to me. I paid them no mind, even with their guns, it didn't faze me. I told them they would be scared to death in prison. You don't get guns there. Even a baby can pull a trigger. That doesn't make you tough. So, no, I wasn't afraid of their guns.

Bobby impressed all the Street Workers, without exception. He was seen as a "great guy" a "standup guy," tough, intimidating, fearless. "The kind of guy you want to go into the trenches with," was how Chris described his workmate. Bobby was universally seen as committed, one who loved his job and showed it every day. They marveled at his lack of bitterness, from what he went through in prison. The gang members knew his story from the news and talk on the street. Bobby had street "cred" like no one else.

In the beginning the program was school- based. Bobby's Jeramiah Burke High School was infested with gangs, estimated to include such rivals as Castlegate, Columbia Point Dogs, the Stonehurst, and Vamp Hill gangs. The latter did not identify with where they were from; rather, what they did: "vamp" was slang for robbery.

"Bobby's MO was to be tough, firm but fair, and always respectful. He addressed the students and gang members as 'young man, young lady' Chris recalls.

Respect was reciprocated. Bobby Joe created relationships that worked well in providing order at the Jerry and continued beyond school hours. He would hunt down students who were truant, knowing exactly where they could be found on the street. He found jobs for them by going right into the big box stores at the shopping malls, searching out the managers, and vouching for those pulling themselves away from gang life. Bobby Joe was there for them 24/7, taking calls from them whenever they needed him, sometimes just to talk about girlfriend issues or problems at home.

One summer, the City funded a program that got jobs for 250 gang members. The Street Workers who monitored them at school or on the streets were responsible for them at the job sites. Even when working, most had one foot still with the gangs, and packed guns for their safety. One day two workers from rival gangs had a beef at the job site. One had a supervisor position, the other was a worker in his crew. Not unpredictably, the one did not take to being told how to do his job by the rival gang supervisor, and a pistol appeared. Bobby did not hesitate to get between them, and he calmed them down without physically attempting to disarm either.

"This is not the way to go" he said.

His words and his presence ended it. The young man with the gun had to be terminated. But he was not forgotten by Bobby, who found other employment, keeping him focused on success and away from his earlier failure.

Tracy Lithcutt joined the Street Worker program one year before Bobby Joe's arrival. He was homegrown as well, coming from Boston's South End. It was the same neighborhood that welcomed Bobby Joe when he moved in with Judy until the welcome wagon turned into a police wagon that carted him off to prison. After his freedom was ordered by the court in November 1986, Bobby moved to the South End with his girlfriend June. It could be said that Bobby Joe was a long time South End resident if you counted his 15 ½ year break in service. Perhaps the South End is a metaphor for Bobby's return to normalcy. It certainly became his home.

An All City and All State forward at Boston Technical High School, Tracy went on to play at Morgan State. Tracy remembers meeting Bobby before his City employment:

"I used to see Bobby in the neighborhood. Everyone learned what happened to him. He became a fixture. He played basketball at Sparrow Park. He belonged. He was part of the South End family."

Tracy shot hoops with his South End neighbor.

When Tracy brought Bobby Joe into the program he became a lifelong best friend. They worked out together with the weights at Mike's Gym, where he observed that "Bobby was ripped. No one on the street would want to mess with him."

Tracy set up speaking engagements for Bobby, mostly in the public high schools, but also at places like the Bridgewater and Framingham State Colleges the Harvard School of Public Health and the Kennedy School of Government. "The purpose was to inspire the students."

Bobby's message of faith and perseverance masked his physical strength and toughness.

"You know, I saw it a few times. Bobby was fearless. The gang members knew he spent almost 16 years in prison. They respected him for that and knew not to mess with someone that looked like Bobby and spent that kind of time in state prison. That was what I call the wrong reason for respect. The right reason was when they learned that Bobby was innocent, was wrongfully convicted. That's when they showed the most respect."

During the troubles, when the bodies of inner-city Black youths were piling up like pancakes, Tracy and Bobby would go to homicide scenes:

"He always had my back. Physically, every way.' Tracy reports. "The gang members were always in the crowd. They were angry if one of their own was shot. Revenge always happened. We would try to calm them down."

Tracy and Bobby often monitored the Boston Marathon in April of each year. The finish line is only a mile from the Brookline border, and while thousands would cheer along the other 25 miles of the running route, the area from Fenway Park to the yellow ribbon that stretched across Boylston Street at the 26.2 mile marker, was compressed with tens of thousands of enthusiastic and sometimes inebriated fans. The dynamic duo kept their eyes on the fans and not the runners. The adage, "a word to the wise is sufficient" comes to mind when Bobby and Tracy would encourage some over- exuberant youth to settle down. But not always:

"I remember one year, we were walking around, and two real assholes had water cannons, and were firing it at people, and could hurt them. So, Bobby stepped up to them and told them to stop. Of course, they didn't and pointed it at Bobby and me. Bobby had one of them on the trunk of a car in seconds before a drop of water was fired. I was ready to punch the other. Bobby said "Stop. Don't hit him." I did as he told me. Nothing more was needed. Nothing more was ever needed with Bobby."

One day, Tracy and Bobby were driving the city van along Blue Hill Ave when they were distracted by two girls whaling two other girls with their fists. The two big body builders stopped the van and interceded.

"I looked over and saw one of the girls hanging from Bobby's shoulders and punching him. But in time they stopped."

Of course, Bobby was too much of a gentleman to hit back.

Showing no fear was vital if a Street Worker wanted to communicate with a gang member and earn his trust. The object was to stop the violence. Their message was that there were better and safer ways of living. Bobby Joe earned their respect, obtained their trust, and found ways to help them. But you could not be afraid of them.

Once Bobby and Tracy went into "Block City" in the

Mission Hill projects, so-called because the city put wooden blocks in an area for little kids to play on. Instead, it became the largest and worst open-air drug market in the city. You could buy anything at Block City; weed, heroin coke, crack, anything. This was the GOYA Gang territory, which in long- hand was *GUNS ON YOUR ASS.* Although they were one of the most violent gangs in Boston, Bobby still engaged with them as he would with any other.

I was speaking to a gang member and asked him why, why were you with the gang? He told me he was in college but dropped out because he needed money. I explained to him that I would get him a job He said yes to that. He would see me in a few days. I gave him my card. We left the area. A few hours later we were told to respond to a scene where a kid was shot and murdered. It was the young man I was trying to save. Tracy and I were both heartbroken. We both cried.

When all the major ministries in the minority neighborhoods loudly proclaimed that enough was enough, that the carnage of the young had to stop, they formed the Ten Point Coalition. The ten points of their plan contained specific goals to reduce violence and provide services to Black and Latino gang members. They would build partnerships with law enforcement that included Boston police, city and federal prosecutors, probation officers and community workers. Their first goal was to stop the shooting, to attempt a ceasefire among the gangs. The Street Worker program was the designated front line for this battle. Bobby Joe and several other streetworkers were the ones that would try to bring it about.

THE VANS

We used vans to drive around the neighborhoods, also to take the young men to job interviews. We drove them to the jobs when we got them. We got to know the families of the gang members, their mothers and fathers, brothers, and sisters. We would meet them on the street sometimes. But mostly we got friendly with them when we went to their homes sometimes just to check up on the young people. Sometimes Tracy made schedules for us. Other times it just happened. But we got to know the families pretty well.

When the holidays came, we got free turkeys and gave them to their families. We had boxes all over Boston to collect toys at

Christmas. We'd drive the vans all over Boston to pick up boxes filled with toys, and we would give them to gang members for their families. Or we would deliver them ourselves.

Tracy had connections with Reebok and Timberland. We'd load up the vans with cartons of boots and sneakers and hand them out to the gang members.

Tracy came up with the idea of getting the gang members to shoot baskets together instead of bullets at each other. That took a little work. Tracy got BU [Boston University] to let us use their gyms.

I'd drive them to BU for basketball. I'd have 6 or 8 young men from Castlegate or Intervale, maybe Orchard Park. and other street workers had other gangs in their vans. I had to frisk them for guns and knives before they got in the vans. They could not bring gym bags where they could put weapons. They could not bring friends to watch in the stands. Then I drove them. They acted just like kids. Laughing. Making jokes.

With Bobby Joe a recruit for Jackson State's basketball team, Tracy a Morgan State player, Chris at Brandeis, the All-American Robin who could wipe the floor with the men, and Junior with his East Boston High sports cred, the Street Worker B-Ball squad was formidable.

This was not the first time the gang members played the *civilians*. A few years earlier Ray Flynn started the Mayor's All Stars. Flynn was an All-American player at Providence College, and according to Junior he could still run and shoot. There was one thing the housing projects had in common: They always surrounded basketball courts. So, the Mayor gathered the athletes from his departments like Parks and Recreation, cops who knew their way around courts other than those with criminal sessions, and others like Tracy and Junior, and challenged the gang members to hoop. Ray still had it. The gang leaders knew they were competing against cops, and the *friggin'* Mayor of Boston. It was surreal.

The Mayor's people organized cookouts around the games and bought time to talk to the gang members. There were folks who would direct them to city departments, that provided education and job training, and a range of counseling services. It was hugely successful.

So, getting them to play basketball against a mayor, or a

coach or a cop or against streetworkers was already a proven event. Getting them to play against the rivals that they stabbed and shot, well that was a challenge. It was perhaps going to require a miracle, and vans.

It worked. They played hard against each other. Sometimes things got a little out of hand, but we managed it. They really liked playing against us, me, Robin, Chops, Chris, and Tracy. They were amazed how good we were. But they mostly played gang against gang, 2 or 3 time a week. They got to be kinda friends with each other.

We gave a name to this program: The Peace League. We got them ready to sit down for a ceasefire.

1010 MASSACHUSETTS AVE

In the early nineties the Street Workers were housed in a six-story municipal building at 1010 Massachusetts Avenue. This is the same street on which Bobby was arrested. The building is three blocks from the City Hospital parking lot where he was mis-identified. It is a heavy industrial area, within earshot of the Southeast Expressway, and was a perfect, *neutral* location to bring gang members for meetings. There were a number of them before the ceasefire agreement was reached.

Chris Byner remembers the lead up to a meeting with the Wendover Street gang of mostly Cape Verdeans, and the Stonehurst, a Black gang from Bowdoin Street in Mattapan. Deputy Superintendent Paul Joyce asked to arrange a face-to-face meeting with the gang leaders as he needed to talk directly to them. He wanted to get a message to them: *the shooting had to stop.*

Because Bobby and his coworkers had forged street level relationships of trust with the gang members, they delivered the invitation, which was accepted by the heavy hitters, the 'influencers,' the gang leaders. Chris remembers the invitation:

"We genuinely wanted them to do well, more importantly to live. It was really life or death. We wanted to help them. Paul Joyce wanted them to hear it from the horse's mouth. Our message was consistent. But we came at it from a different angle. It was the carrot and the stick. We told them this shit has to stop. If you don't ceasefire you're fucked."

Tracy Lithcutt, Bobby Joe, Chris Womart, and Chris Byner

brought the gang leaders into the building. Ironically, many were looking for a way out of the gang-war violence. They sat around a conference table, adults on one side and four or five leaders, or *influencers*, as Chris Byner described the gang representatives who would bring the message back to their neighborhoods, on the other side.

Deputy Superintendent Paul Joyce was present, and he spoke clearly:

"The shooting has to stop. We will give you time to get the gospel to your gang members."

Police used to look the other way for minor offenses like public drinking or driving without a license. Those days were over:

"Police will be all over you, with probation officers ready to surrender you and federal   prosecutors willing to bring federal charges."

Deputy Joyce was speaking about the authority of probation officers to bring before the court defendants who violated the terms of their probation for sanctions that included incarceration. The *Surrender* process was quick, and the only proof required was that the individual, for example, committed another crime, came up dirty on a drug test, failed to report, or simply did not observe the hours of a curfew. Two PO s in the Dorchester Court ingeniously initiated a program called Operation Night Light where they accompanied police on after work patrols, often visiting the apartments where the probationers lived for unannounced "home visits." If they spotted a probationer on the street or not at home, they could arrest him for violation of curfew. Billy Stewart and his partner Richard Skinner quickly got the attention of gang members who use to think probation was a cake walk. Partnering with the police gave them security to go into dangerous situations. Partnering with probation gave the police the ability to keep gang members off the street. It was immediately impactful: Curfew violations spiked and the offenders generally got the message to comply with all the orders of the court.

Going "Fed" was a chilling moment for a gang member arrested by the city cops, for charges involving drugs or firearms, where there was joint jurisdiction with the federal authorities. Boston Police had cooperation agreements with the U. S. Attorney that allowed the transfer of certain cases to the Justice department for prosecution. Going "Fed" meant stiffer mandatory sentences and prisons hundreds of miles away from friends and families in other states, indeed different time zones. One famous instance of "going Fed" involved a gang member who foolishly ignored the *Gospel of St. Paul Joyce.* He brazenly and tauntingly waved a single, but very unlawful, bullet at a Gang Unit officer who was patrolling in a gang area. Because of multiple previous convictions, he faced and received a mandatory 20-year sentence for being a felon in possession of ammunition. The message went out that the Boston Police had a *stick* and were prepared to wield it.

But then, there was the *carrot.* The Street Workers would continue to provide job placement, education opportunities, counseling, and many other services: That was the deal. They organized to work collaboratively with the police to target specific areas where shootings took place. Because they knew the players, their information helped police to monitor activity in designated locations.

Gradually communication went from simple conversations on the streets to group meetings that were scheduled at off hours at the Roxbury, West Roxbury, and Dorchester courthouses. Assistant district attorneys, probation officers, anti-gang police, and the gang members could meet on neutral and protected turf to keep the dialogue open and peace on the streets within reach.

The Street Workers were the critical link to getting everyone in one room to talk. Bobby and his partners drove the young men to and from the courthouses. It guaranteed they attended and protected them from rivals who might learn their schedules. Texting was the new technology, though it was still in its infancy. Bobby, Chris, Tracy, Robin, and the other Street Workers were their shields.

Progress was being made.

OPERATION CEASEFIRE

Junior went on to Direct *City Year,* a service program for young people between high school and college that began in Boston and went national. Next, he held several public service positions before he founded BASE, a sports-oriented education and youth service program working with hundreds of inner-city youth, in a building just two blocks from 1010 Mass Ave. Baseball is very much part of the curriculum, but the program name has little to do with running bases: BASE means, foundation, as in *foundation for the rest of your life.* He remains involved in the mission of the program that began with a ragtag group of young, funny, deadly serious, streetwise and generous souls who helped redefine street justice in Boston. Tracy stayed on the streets until he became Public Safety director with Mayor Marty Walsh. Chris and Robin continued to work every day with Bobby.

The "Operation Ceasefire" halt to youth homicides was broken after 27 months, but the rate of killings remained low through the nineties. When Junior left, Tracy took over, following the early formula: "We were the medicine for cancer," Tracy recalls. They were going to keep treating the disease and hope for a cure. It was all based on partnerships. The "carrot" was with the clergy, city wide community programs, businesses, and philanthropists. The "stick" was the police, probation officers, and prosecutors. These were the Street Workers' partners.

Tracy saw the program grow under his watch, increasing to 60 or 70 workers, with a good mix. About 60% had college degrees, 20 % had some college, 10% had attended high school, and 10 % were ex-cons. They each had a different way of relating. Funding came easily, and Tracy was able to spread the new workers throughout the critical neighborhoods and beyond. Some were assigned to the clergy, like the Reverends Rivers, Hammond, and Wall. Bruce Wall had a crisis response unit. They were constantly looking for different ways to manage the problems.

The vans kept running through the dangerous streets of gang turf. As Tracy recalls, "We got hundreds of Patriots tickets and Celtics tickets. We kept some and distributed the rest to other civic groups. Bobby Joe passed them out with sweatshirts to the gang members and the good kids too. "

"What we needed was resources and being creative."

They were now placing 500 gang members in summer jobs, and they saw a reduction in summertime violence. Tracy observed: "They couldn't stay out all night and do dumb stuff when they had to work next morning."

During the school year, his workers went back to walking the halls in the high schools, breaking up altercations, and cajoling them to stay in the classrooms. They put two workers in the worst schools, which always included Bobby Joe and usually meant going to Dorchester High or the Burke, because Tracy adds:

"Bobby was a star. He got instant respect, and he would get right into a fray if he had to. He was tough. But they also helped guys get into alternative education and connected them with jobs. The Street Workers would go to the sporting events, basketball games etc. They liked having them there to keep the game safe. Kids felt comfortable going to them."

And then again, there was the stick. Their success depended on a trusting relationship with the police and the courts. Tracy saw major change from the stop and frisk days to Community Policing. Their partnership involved a department wide shift in community relations and resulted in all police officers being se to the Boston Police Academy for retraining. Tracy and other Street Workers participated in that training. That is where the partnerships developed best.

Tracy cannot underestimate the critical value of teaming up with the local courts, especially the Dorchester Court, its Presiding Justice Sydney Hanlon, and Chief Probation Officer Bernard Fitzgerald, or as he was more frequently named, "Bernie Fitz".

"I stopped having cases, but I was interested in one young man whom I brought to court and seated in the crowd area. Judge Hanlon saw me and called me up to the bench, making a big deal of seeing me and asking how I was doing. Then they called my case first, and I asked for a second or third chance for a young man because I thought he deserved it. I don't know what the DA said, but Judge Hanlon did as I requested, and my man did not go to jail. They continued his probation. I walked back and all these mothers of gang members and other defendants asked *"Can I have your card? Can I have your card?"*

"Bobby Joe got treated the same way. If he told Bernie Fitz or the judge that his man deserved another chance, they always gave it because they respected Bobby's recommendations. They trusted Bobby. If Bobby or I didn't think they deserved it, we would not show up. That way we kept our credibility with the courts and the kids."

The assistant DA in charge of the gang unit at that time was Bob Tochka.

"He was careful with us in the beginning, but then he was wonderful. We could talk with him about getting extra chances for our guys that deserved it. He respected our opinions a lot."

Bob frequently gave up his evenings at home with family,

to attend group meetings usually with his wingman, ADA Raffi Yessayan, that were scheduled at the Roxbury, West Roxbury, and Dorchester courthouses. When Bob was appointed to the Boston Municipal Court he gave the same measured treatment to the Street Worker clients. He went on to the Superior Court and became a leader in promoting real value probation and alternatives to incarceration. Raffi, who was a law student intern with me and my brother Pete, joined him on the Superior Court.

The success of the Street Worker program can be measured in several ways. First, it received enormous attention from academia and from other cities. Former Attorney General Janet Reno came to Boston to learn about the program, as did law enforcement representatives from across the country. Editorial Boards praised it and politicians glowed in its success. And the ultimate metric? Google quickly connects to the search words, The Boston Miracle.

Boston Mayor Ray Flynn stood side by side with Bobby Joe in many hot spots in the city. The late Mayor Tom Menino stated that "Mayors come and go but there are only a few Bobby Joe's." Mayor Marty Walsh publicly identified Bobby as a City of Boston treasure.

COMMUNITY POLICE PAYBACK

On March 25, 1994, the war on drugs produced one more innocent casualty, and threatened the trust and good will being established by the Boston Police.

75-year-old Accelyne Williams was a retired pastor who had recently moved to Dorchester from the Caribbean to be closer to his daughter. In mid-afternoon, a fully armed Boston Police SWAT team knocked in the door of his apartment and chased Rev. Williams into a bedroom. He was tossed to the ground and handcuffed, and as he struggled, he had a fatal heart attack. The Medical examiner noted that he expired within minutes. The death shocked the city, and once again enraged the Black community.

Detectives had learned from an informant that drug dealers had stored two kilos of cocaine and high-power firearms, including at least one machine gun, in a second-floor apartment in Dorchester and planned on removing the drugs and weapons that evening. The informant had given good information in the past and confirmed that he had actually seen the contraband two days earlier.

He travelled with a detective to the alleged drug site. He pointed with his finger upward from an unmarked car, saying, "There, the second floor." This information was put in an affidavit signed by the lead detective, and under the direction of an Assistant District Attorney, was attached to a search warrant application. A judge reviewed the documents and issued a search warrant, which because of a high possibility of violence, provided a "No Knock" provision."

The SWAT team assembled and was briefed on the particulars. They expected to find four heavily armed Jamaican drug dealers and prepared accordingly with Kevlar body armor and their own assault weapons. Instead, when they rammed through the front door of the apartment, they found an innocent man of God. The drug dealers were on the third floor, and escaped detection.

The expression, "the shit hit the fan" comes to mind as I recall the phone call I received from Tommy Montgomery directing me to the Homicide Unit in South Boston, to make sure questioning of the detectives was done fairly. The Homicide Unit had jurisdiction because it was a sudden death investigation. Cops could be charged with crimes. They could, as it happened, be charged with violations of regulations and procedures and face discipline including suspension and termination. Three detectives were charged with neglect of duty relating to the issuance and the supervision of the issuance of search warrants. For the next two years, I plodded through highly charged and publicized administrative hearings and an appeal to state Civil Service.

In the aftermath, city and police officials got ahead of the crisis by going into the community and answering questions. Police Commissioner Paul Evans and Mayor Tom Menino attended meetings in the Codman Square section of Dorchester and put the information out: The police went to the wrong apartment; Reverend Williams tragically died; They and the city grieve for them. They would not walk away from their culpability or their responsibility to compensate the family for their loss.

I was acquainted with the Reverend Bruce Wall who worked in the Boston Juvenile Court and had an active street ministry in Dorchester. Bruce hit the streets and got in front of microphones. He, and other members of the clergy urged calm and restraint. The incident could have blown up the improved relationship they had developed with the police department; It did not. The work of the Ten Point Coalition and especially the Street Workers would continue.

The newspapers reported on the "bungled drug raid." In fact, it was caused by human error and not police misconduct. The informant, also from the Caribbean, numbered the floors of a building as "Ground floor, First Floor, Second Floor" etc.as is the custom in many cultures. When he pointed and described the second floor, he was referring to what we signify as the third floor.

But there was a death, and the wheels of administrative justice grind slowly and sometimes unfairly. My client, a popular and well-regarded Lieutenant Detective was suspended for thirty days. As he was close to retirement age, he turned in his papers and moved to Maine. Two years later he was vindicated by Civil Service which affirmatively found he did not neglect his duty and ordered his back pay of $7000.00.

It is an axiom of the law, and an immediately understood personal feeling, that no amount of money can compensate the family for the loss of a life cherished by them. But the city and Reverend Williams' survivors did agree on a settlement, avoiding the delay and rancor of litigation.

And the very important new and growing trusting relationship of the minority community with the Boston Police Department was preserved...at least for a time.

ANSWERING MY CALLING

One winter morning in 1999, I was waiting for a case to be called in the Boston Municipal Court, one of my many "most favorite" courts. The BMC had a vibrancy like no other city court. It was a clearing house for major and minor crimes committed in downtown Boston. The serious ones were generally indicted and promptly removed to the Superior Court. The minor ones remained, and many played out like scenes from Judge Judy and *Night Court*. My cases usually involved stupid behavior from otherwise decent members of society, which is another way of saying they could afford to pay for my services. Most involved the consumption of alcohol and activity behind the wheel of a car or inside a bar. I forget the circumstance of my lawyering that day, but I remember well the rest of that morning.

Jay Carney, Mark Devlin's prosecutor and my friend, was

also waiting for a case to be called in the arraignment session of the BMC. The delay was interminable. There had to be a hundred cases on the docket that day and both Jay and I were at the end. So, when the morning recess was announced, it was a good time to get some fresh air. I offered to buy Jay coffee at the Plaza Deli across from the courthouse.

As we strolled away from the courthouse, Jay reminded me that he was a member of the Judicial Nominating Commission, the JNC, the committee of about twenty lawyers who interview and recommend candidates for nomination as judges. I responded with a comment like, "That's great, Jay. Good to have guys like you on it." He noted that Governor Paul Cellucci had a different philosophy for appointment than his predecessor Bill Weld.

"He's not as interested in federal prosecutors and members of white shoe law firms."

Coming from the Bromfield Street establishment, where we worked in running shoes, I told him, "That's an improvement." As we moved along the deli line to pay up, I nearly sprayed out the coffee I was sipping when Jay said, "And I think you, Chris, would be perfect for the Superior Court." The customary response to this former chairman of the JNC would be something to the effect, "What an Honor, What a privilege." I blurted out, "You gotta be shittin' me."

Jay has a lovely way with jurors, persuasive without being argumentative, soft-spoken but very clear. That was his manner and tone as he convinced me to "at least, just get the application a few blocks away at the State House. Then call me." I agreed.

For the next six months, I reviewed case files going back twenty years, to identify judges and opposing counsel, and filled out all the details of my personal and professional life. The lengthy application went through eight re-writes. In August that year I got sick of the process and called it quits with the most recent iteration, made twenty-five copies, and placed each in a large envelope addressed to the individual members of the JNC. I brought the stack to my Cape Cod post office, said good riddance to them, and continued on to the harbor for a boat ride.

Then, I waited. And then, I waited some more.

It was a year before I was invited for an interview before the whole panel. Jack Moscardelli was the chairman and said, "Here's an easy question: Why do you want to be a Superior Court

Judge, and why should the Governor appoint you?"

My answers flowed fairly well until one member asked why I listed as a reference U.S. Army General George W. Casey Jr.

On the application there was a place to list five character witnesses. Most applicants, I learned, identified lawyers and judges. I listed people who were well regarded in the larger community, and who knew me for a long time. General George was my college roommate and close friend. He went on to become the longest serving commander of the forces in Iraq, and then Chief of Staff of the Army. I wanted to warn him about a possible reference request, so I called a number with a Georgia area code. There was a long delay until George finally answered. He told me it was early morning in Bosnia, and his security detail went to his bunker to bring him to the communications center where my call to Georgia had been rerouted. Naturally I apologized for the inconvenience of interrupting a war zone, but I pressed George to indicate *what* he would say about me. He answered:

"If I can be a General, you can be a Judge. Now I'm going back to bed."

I recounted that episode to the inquiring member. My interview was over, and I began another long, long wait.

I was sworn in as an Associate Justice of the Massachusetts Superior Court on May 18, 2001, which coincidentally was Karen's birthday. I joined 80 other Justices who, as was their history and custom, welcomed me with support, kindness, and friendship. As a lawyer, I felt comfortable in court rooms throughout the state, confident in my understanding of the law, rules of evidence, and trial procedures. But as a judge, well, I brought a lot of healthy skepticism of my ability to serve in that role. I would not make the common mistake of believing that the skills of a lawyer were interchangeable with those of a judge.

The best advice I received was when I went to the Dedham Superior Court to clean up a pending case. After I was nominated I had a few weeks to withdraw from cases and to wrap up my law office business. I went to see the Clerk, Walter Timilty, who helped me file some routine paperwork. Then he asked me to come with him to the judge's lobby to visit with Elizabeth Butler. I resisted, as I was sure she was too busy, and I did not want to interrupt her work. He insisted, "She would love to meet you." Walter was right: As I learned, and as I came to practice, sitting judges are a welcoming committee to the newly appointed. Beth, as I would later call her, was exuberant with her "Hello, Welcome. Come in. Let's talk." She mentioned three things that I have remembered and often repeated to new judges.

"Do you have kids?" she asked. When I answered affirmatively, she said, 'Wonderful, this job is great for families. You'll have a predictable schedule which lawyers never have. You can take vacations and not worry about clients. And you have judges who will cover for you."

"Is it too isolating, being a judge?" I asked. "Only if you make it. Don't tell people you're a judge and you can have a normal life."

Then without prompting she said, "The hardest part of being a judge is with bails and sentencing." It was not until I was deciding if and how long I would take away the liberty of a defendant appearing before me, that I understood the wisdom of Beth's words.

THE GREAT TRIAL COURT
OF THE COMMONWEALTH

The Massachusetts Superior Court has jurisdiction over major felonies, those crimes which provide for a state prison sentence, civil cases with claims over $50,000, and requests for equitable relief.

Equity was designed to fill in the blanks for cases that required relief that the Law sometimes could not accommodate. For example, if a home was to be auctioned because of a claimed mortgage default, the homeowner needed immediate court intervention. If there was good cause, a court would halt the sale, if not, the auction could proceed. I had many cases that needed immediate attention. They included agreements not to compete where former employees could possibly injure the businesses they were leaving, that would be balanced with their need to continue to earn a living. The financial meltdown of 2008 brought hundreds of mortgage foreclosures to our courthouse doors. I had to rule for example, on whether a well-known author could publish her memoir over the objection of a former boyfriend who was not presented very sympathetically; a contractor frozen out of a job by public bidding rules; a Native American denied shell fishing in ancient tribal waters; a bar owner contesting a seven-day license suspension; a sex offender objecting to a registration requirement; and dozens of claims by citizens who would face irreparable harm if the court did not intercede. I was asked by a town health agent to order a homeowner to remove hogs and other animals from a residential area because of offensive olfactory hazards – the animals stunk up the neighborhood. I ordered the owner to get rid of the hogs and all other animals except his pet billy goat named Stinky Bill. Despite his name, it was proven he did not present a hazard to the nose.

Most of my civil work involved business, homeowner, manufacturer, contractor, and municipal disputes and claims of personal injury, from fender benders to tragic wrongful deaths. I always recognized that each case was important to the litigant and tried to facilitate justice patiently and soundly. That is not to say I always succeeded: However, I can say that I always maintained that objective, and nearly always tried.

I recall attending a conference with some out of state judges after less than a year on the bench. The spouse of a Michigan judge asked me what I liked most about my new position, then answered her own question before I could: "It's the power, right?" I thought a moment and came back, "No. I don't see it as power. Judges have responsibility. Lawyers have all the power."

The most difficult cases before a Superior Court Justice involve criminal indictments. My more cerebral colleagues may disagree, and suggest that complex commercial litigation, or some other area in the civil trial sessions, is more demanding and filled with Olympic sized legal issues that test the very intellectual mettle of the judge. My simple response is: They are wrong.

I never forgot the advice, or warning, of Judge Beth Butler that bails and sentencing were the most difficult parts of the Judge's job. Judges preside over trials of individuals who both act violently and who suffer from that violence. Victims include the family and friends of the complaining witnesses and the family and friends of the defendant. A slow-moving murder, sexual assault, arson, or armed robbery trial fills a courtroom with exhibits and testimony that narrates the underlying tragedy of the criminal events. The professionals in the room, lawyers, clerks, court officers, and the judge wear faces of dispassionate interest and show no emotion. But they all feel the pain as it emerges from the mouths of witnesses. Empathy can be masked, but it is not suppressed.

After a jury returns a guilty verdict, the victims are invited to provide an impact statement. These are powerful moments, and those reports of the permanent loss and injury felt by those who suffered from the crimes, are often indelible. The lawyers who plead for their clients will often remark that the crime should not define the entirety of the defendant's life, especially those crimes that did not involve acts of violence. The judge is left to balance fairly those often divergent views.

It is then that the judge must decide a fair and just sentence. If it calls for imprisonment, it begs the question, how long? What length of time will provide deterrence, punishment, public safety, and possible rehabilitation? Optimally it should be neither a day more, nor a day less. In Massachusetts we have non-mandatory sentencing guidelines which provide a range of options. The federal system was once burdened with intractable mandatory sentencing guidelines that did more to promote mass incarceration that any other criminal justice policy. Those guidelines took away the discretion of judges to formulate just sentences. One federal judge in Boston, Edward Harrington, declined to judge any future criminal cases because, as he noted, his responsibility to see that justice was done was appropriated by the prosecutor when the charges were decided. When mandatory guidelines were substantially undercut by the U.S. Supreme Court, Judge Harrington returned to the criminal sessions by way of a court memorandum which stated his reasons, and which I often included in my sentencing memoranda:

> *The Court shall handle the sentencing as courts handled sentencing before the Guidelines—by making a full examination of an individual defendant's personal character, family responsibilities, medical and mental condition, criminal record, and the particular circumstances surrounding the crime and imposing an appropriate sentence within the broad range set by Congress, after deep reflection informed by the experience in life and in the law.*

Now that I am retired and a bit reflective, I view prosecutors who insisted on lengthy sentences because, transparently, *more time was a win*, as having created reputations that will haunt them in later years. Fairness and sound judgment are attributes in the legal profession that are respected. I often told prosecutors that their estimate of a fair sentence should approximate mine—we shared the same interests in protecting the public, deterring crime, and punishing the guilty. Some of them listened to me; others blew me off, not unlike the way I did with judges when I was in my twenties.

On my 70th birthday in August 2018, I accepted mandatory retirement with a great deal of reluctance but with no regrets. I wrote a farewell note to all of my brothers and sisters on the bench and told them that for seventeen years, I never had a bad day, and every day was a great one. It is the rule of law that guides a just society. It was my luck, my good fortune, to find a life in the law, and to promote that great objective. It was also a boatload of fun.

FOR THE YOUNG PEOPLE

For nearly thirty years high school students from Boston have been invited to participate in the Judicial Youth Corps. Each spring two dozen junior class members will come to the administrative offices of the Supreme Judicial Court and meet Vanessa Scott Woodbury who will become their den mother as they attend sessions offered by volunteer lawyers, judges, clerks, and court personnel who instruct them on the Rule of Law. Vanessa is a no-nonsense woman who has no limits of motherly attention, or as might be required, unrelenting tough love, for her summertime charges. She monitors their attendance at the sessions and later, as they are paired with court employees for full time paid internships, keeps a watchful eye on their progress. The program has been a life changer, as the students head back to every high school in the city with confidence and ambition. Many attend college, a few graduate from law school, others find positions in the trades, professions, and business. One became a state senator. None of this success would have been possible without the support of her assistant, Jerry Howland.

I met Jerry in September 1972 during the evening orientation program put on by Suffolk Law School. We were both Boston schoolteachers. Jerry planned on getting his degree and then starting a law practice. As I often note, I hoped to remain a classroom teacher, with a law degree as an insurance policy. Our ambitions reversed, as Jerry not only stayed in the classroom after graduation and passing the Bar exam, but became nationally recognized, and (he will hate this comment) for decades was the premier educator in Boston. He also mentored dozens of students, indeed rescuing more than a few from desperate circumstances. At the 25th anniversary celebration of the creation of the JYC I heard from dozens, among the hundreds, of program graduates who credited their success to their life-changing summer with Jerry and the JYC.

Each summer Vanessa and Jerry invited Bobby Joe and me to present during one of the scheduled afternoon sessions. Big Bob participated until his death in 2012. The first one was most memorable as Chief Justice Liacos interrupted it to meet Bobby and apologize to him for the miscarriage of justice he suffered.

Jerry introduced Bobby the same way every year:

"Some have heroes like Michael Jordan, or Ted Williams, who was mine when I was your age. My hero is Bobby Joe Leaster."

Bobby, Jerry Howland, and the First Team, final time together, speaking to Judicial Youth Corp,

At the end of the session the students generally understand Jerry and unanimously share his view.

Most of the kids look like Bobby, many come from the neighborhood streets that Bobby "walks" and everyone becomes spellbound as they listen to his narrative. They question how it was possible that he was convicted, that he could have been executed, and that he was imprisoned for 15 1/2 years. They are most startled by Bobby's explanation to their predictable question: Why aren't you bitter?

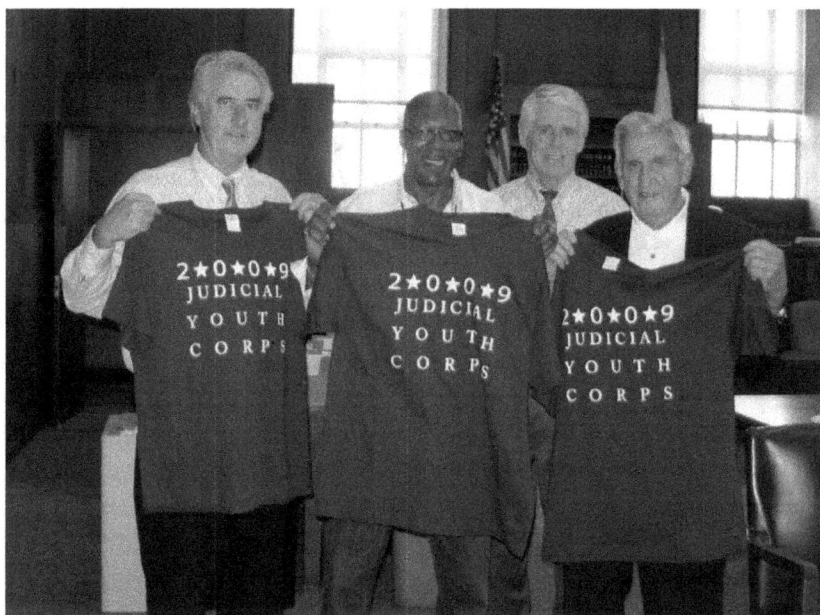

I still speak a lot to the kids. Every year, now it's over 25 years, I speak with Chris and Jerry Howland at the Judicial Youth Corp, and used to with Mr. Muse before he passed, in the Suffolk County Courthouse. The same place that found me guilty of murder and sent me off to Walpole. I always tell them the same thing: that God saved me, that God sent me the Muses, that you have to have faith and hope, and that you can't become bitter. Every year at least one student asks me, why am I not bitter? I always answer the same. I don't have time to be bitter. I'm glad to be free. Being bitter will put me back in prison. I started my life over when I was 36. I know what they did to me was wrong. I like my life, I love my life, and I look forward to my future.

When people, like the kids, ask me I tell them that I would not change any part of my life, including my wrongful conviction and spending 15 ½ years in prison for a crime I did not commit. I tell them I never would have met the Muses or Mr. Howland or all the people I help with my job.

Every June when I go to speak with Chris and Jerry Howland, it's only a happy time. It is a blessed time.

FAITH

I didn't just work with gang members even during the ceasefire. There were lots of young people that didn't belong to gangs that needed help. The city had summer jobs programs and we used to line them up before school got out. I went to the jails to help the people leaving Suffolk jail to find jobs. I returned to Norfolk a lot to speak with the prisoners there, to give them hope on the outside. Sometimes I'd see kids from the streets that I warned about getting out of the gangs or they'd end up in prison. They'd come up to me and say I was right, sometimes with tears in their eyes, and say they wished they listened to me.

We had a funeral squad to go to the funerals of young people killed on the streets. It hasn't stopped. It's gotten worse. I think I have been to over 800. Sometimes two or three times a week. Sometimes two in the same day. We go to keep peace, and to pay our respects. I usually knew the deceased. I usually knew the gang, sometimes the gang member who shot him. It tears my heart apart.

For the past years I have been assigned to the MBTA to help their security keep peace at the train stations when the young people got out of school. They all know me. I can walk up to a group that might be getting ready to fight and I can cool them down. They listen to me.

My son is now over thirty. I haven't lived with his mother for a long time. But we both stay friends and made sure RJ grew up right. June made sure he got into all the right schools, like the METCO program that sent him to Newton just outside of Boston. He graduated from Newton North High School and then went to college in New Hampshire. I set aside a large part of my money from the state to pay his tuition. He did really well. He has a job at Children's Hospital working with computers. He knows my whole story.

I still attend church a lot. Faith is still important to me. I know God is still directing my life. I pray every morning. I always pray for my mother and dad, and for Mr. Muse and Chris' mother. I know God is listening to me.

I am getting ready to retire from the Street Workers. I almost have thirty years with the City, and I can get a full pension. I think every day I was on the street I was doing work for God. I love my life, what it became. If I didn't get arrested and have that tragedy, maybe I wouldn't be a Street Worker or meet all the people I have or helped the young people. I know there is not enough justice out there, so I try to bring justice to the streets. I don't just tell gang members not to shoot others; to treat them with respect. I think respect is another word for justice sometimes. If you respect everyone you won't hurt them or do them pain. You treat them fairly; you don't take advantage of them. I try to help them. I tell them to stay in school. To go to college or get some training for a job to make a lot of money. Don't be roaming the streets with nothing to do. And, if someone tries to get you into a gang, stay away from them.

Their parents sometimes know who I am. They tell them my story. I get questions from them, like, Do I believe in God? I tell them that I have faith that the man up above is watching over them. I tell them, He works in mysterious ways, but He is always there for you.

I have been working with the police and probation officers and judges since I started with the Street Workers. That is very strange. I never would have thought this could happen when I was doing life for murder. Now when I bring a young man to the Dorchester Court to help them out, everyone asks, "Bobby, can this young man be saved?" I answer yes and he gets a second chance. I have done this hundreds of times in the same courtroom where I was arraigned after I got arrested and sent to jail until my people raised my bail after two weeks.

I think I bring God to everyone in the court. I think they all know God should be looking over their work. I guess I remind them.

In Memoriam

I could never imagine that Bobby Joe Leaser would die before our story was told.

After I retired as a Judge, Bobby would remind me that he was not far behind. He had little more than a year before he hit the 30-year mark for full retirement benefits, and then he would go out speaking with me full time about *"my case."*

Late afternoon on April 5, 2020, Bobby returned to the two-bedroom apartment in Mattapan that he shared with his son RJ. He had two luxuries he indulged himself: men's cologne and candles. As he was lying down on his couch, a scented candle he recently lit somehow came into contact with a blanket, creating a conflagration that enveloped him. Firefighters responded promptly but too late. He was taken by ambulance to Brigham and Women's Hospital and treated for severe burns over most of his body.

When I heard the news, I was in shock. I made uncountable calls to family and friends. Social media buzzed with the news as his friends and fellow workers Facebooked and Instagrammed their pain. I reached out to RJ and started a daily correspondence through the three weeks leading up to his passing.

Mark Gillespie, a Lieutenant on the MBTA police force where Bobby was detailed for ten years, cried with me as he recounted how every morning Bobby came into his office to start their days with his big smile and discussion about where Bobby would travel to keep the peace on the subways. Tracy Litthcut was now the director of the office of Public Safety in Boston, and shadowed RJ throughout the next month and beyond. We three reached out to everyone who knew Bobby and asked for their prayers. Mark started a prayer chain: I ordered a thousand yellow wrist bands that said *God Bless Bobby Joe* which Mark and Tracy distributed. Prayers were offered by nuns in convents and priests in downtown churches. A week into his hospitalization, Bobby showed signs of progress with his vital organs, and hope and expressions of hope were exchanged. And then, the decline.

RJ telephoned me around noon on a Sunday and told me he was called to come to his dad's bedside. This was the beginning of the Covid 19 pandemic and hospitals were closed to everyone except patients and health care providers. Family visits were not permitted, except like in these circumstances, when a single family member could say goodbye. RJ had earlier communicated with his dad by having a nurse hold a phone to the ear of Bobby Joe, his body completely wrapped like a mummy with bandages and gauze, as RJ told his nonresponding father how much he was loved. Now he could speak to him at his bedside as his spirit noticeably faded away.

When I reached the hospital, I did everything to get permission to go to my friend's bedside. I asked the front desk to let me take RJ's place for a few minutes. After flattery and unsuccessful begging, I told the nurse that I would try to sneak up the back stairs, *but* I would make sure I did not get her in trouble. She smiled and lifted her finger pointing it to the chairs in the waiting area. I sat there calling friends who had friends who might know someone to get me to the ICU floor. Of course, because of Covid, it was all in vain. But the nurses on the floor who were aware of my concern, came downstairs to me to explain that Bobby was getting care and love and that, maybe not in these exact words, "time was running out." I appreciated their thoughtfulness.

At 2:50 PM, my heart started racing almost out of control causing me to stand up to walk about and breathe slowly. My anxiety attack foreshadowed a nurse and an orderly pushing a wailing RJ on a wheelchair towards me in the waiting area, because shortly after 3:00 PM on April 26 my brother's heart stopped beating. I wrapped my arms around RJ and kissed him and kept repeating that he meant everything to his dad, that Bobby Joe wanted his freedom to have a child and that no one made him prouder than his son.

The next day Mayor Marty Walsh interrupted his daily Covid 19 news conference to announce the tragic news. He reminded his viewers that Bobby mentored hundreds of kids all over Boston who faced difficulties and dangers in their lives. He loved the city and the city loved him back. He asked for a moment of silence in his memory.

Only 10 people were allowed at the funeral, so the services were Zoomed by a friend of RJ. I was honored to deliver a eulogy, that recounted the journey of this saint from Reform Alabama. The *Boston Globe* columnist, Kevin Cullen aptly stated that Bobby Joe Leaster was the Mandela of Boston, and wrote:

When the pandemic lifts, they will hold a proper memorial

service for Bobby Joe Leaster, attended by dozens of people who work for a criminal justice system that failed him then felt his embrace, and by dozens of men who never heard a steel door shut behind them because a good son of Alabama decided to make Boston his home.

Bobby's casket was carried out of the funeral home and placed in a hearse that led a procession of cars filled with mourners who could not attend the services, that drove from Mattapan through Roxbury and up to the top of Mission Hill. There, Bobby Joe's co-workers crowded the steps of the Boston Center for Youth and Families and held signs expressing their love and their grief. The cortege continued to Bobby Joe's final resting place in Mount Hope Cemetery. It is a short distance from his Mattapan home and a long way from Reform Alabama.

Epilogue

VOICES FOR JUSTICE

Bobby's passing left me sad and angry. His life, interrupted by gross injustice, and his death, marked by a final breath exhaled from a charred body, tested the limits of my faith in a just God. That was me; it was not Bobby. I knew with certainty that Bobby's faith would have strengthened if he had survived, and if he was conscious of a pending death, as he likely was, he would have accepted it as part of the plan of the Good Master above us.

His death was a powerful kick in my gut. I was burdened by a resistance to see anything beyond a horrible tragedy and an unfair assault on a perfect human being. I dealt with my grief like so many others who have suddenly lost a loved one, starting with confusion and hopelessness, then to acceptance with sorrow, and finally to a less painful memory of a life well lived.

Writing this book was my therapy. It allowed me to focus on every part of Bobby Joe's life-his struggles of course, but also the majority of moments we shared together in friendship, and especially when we talked about "my case." Mostly this exercise of writing caused me to ask more questions than I can answer on the subject that is the title.

While *Justice* directed by *God-* or for the more secular, *by The Creator*, has many guideposts and as many mysteries, the *Justice* promoted by humans is more manageable. When I was a freshman at Georgetown, I read *Plato's Republic* and developed that cocky know -it- all attitude of one who *dangerously* had a little knowledge. I could discuss how Socrates framed the topic of justice around questions like *Who is a just man?* and would continue with questions that obscured what the reader first understood with clarity. It was good practice as I now read decisions of our Federal Appellate and Supreme Courts, which sometimes appear to be riddles, with logic sometimes muddied by soothsayers searching for original intent to solve 21st century issues of justice.

Over time I have learned that *Justice* should not be an abstract ideal, and that there is a somewhat clear path to it. I draw guidance from Bobby Joe's life and struggles. From him we can easily identify *injustice*: in Reform- racism, segregation, unequal educational and economic opportunity, no rule of law for Black people; and in Boston, a different brand of racism, but one that denied Bobby Joe fair treatment by police, prosecutors, and the courts. So, as Socrates might ask *What is justice,* inviting difficult responses, we, today, can ask *What is injustice,* and can look to Bobby's life to identify it, and our life experiences and our good will to address it.

Soon after Bobby Joe died, Jerry Howland emailed dozens of Boston school kids who listened to Bobby Joe's words. One response to Bobby's death eloquently summed up the feelings of all the others:

Bobby wasn't only admired but revered throughout this community by so many young people, and it is heart-wrenching to see him go. The JYC will forever remember him and how he touched each and every one of us in his own special way.

I paused to think of the hundreds of "young people" who listened to his life struggles and his message of caring for each other. He chose to help everyone, and his message was a gift to the widest swath of listeners, from the gang members on mean streets to college and law school students on plush campuses. He had generational appeal– After speaking to my daughter Haley's sixth grade class, the students voted to invite him to their approaching graduation. My youngest son initiated a speaking engagement at Hingham High School and beamed when Bobby gave a shout out to "my brother Jack." Bobby made himself available to everyone and every cause. He did not just refuse to walk away from someone who could benefit from him, he went looking for them. And, he had a message; and the message was about justice. His words, coming from his magical voice, will be missed by countless "young people."

I recall one of my last conversations with him, as he reminded me of the Sermon on the Mount and the Golden Rule: *I don't just tell gang members not to shoot others. I tell them they must love them. I tell them, not to hug them or anything, but to treat them with respect. I think respect is another word for justice sometimes.*

Within days of Bobby's passing, Radha Natarajan from the New England Innocence Project, reached out to me with condolences and an offer to honor Bobby's memory. One "memory" was how Bobby and his case influenced progress in the criminal justice system. She wrote:

"Bobby Joe Leaster's wrongful conviction has many lessons for those of us working in the criminal legal system, some of which have been realized and others that remain to be seen. Having spent 15 years in prison for a crime he did not commit, his case became one of the first in Massachusetts to demonstrate how eyewitness and investigative mistakes are not easily detected or fixed through our appellate courts. His exoneration was critical in underscoring why Massachusetts should not reinstate the death penalty, an irreversible punishment that relies on the unreachable ideal of a flawless system.

"Bobby Joe Leaster will continue to teach us how we can improve our legal system to prevent innocent people like him from being in prison."

A few months later, Radha asked Geraldine Hines and me to offer an in-memoriam introduction to their next scheduled annual awards night the following December. The retired Supreme Judicial Court Justice became friends with Bobby through the predictable means through me and through the courts, but also from coincidentally working out together at a neighborhood gym. Theirs was a warm and familial relationship.

I met Gerri for the first time when we both were being interviewed for judicial appointments, and she walked out a door and into a waiting area belonging to Governor Cellucci's Chief Legal Counsel. Our appointments to the Superior Court were announced on the same day. Later, we partnered in the same courtroom where I learned that the Prophet Micah was her true *Muse,* the one, as the cutout on our bench noted, that inspired her *to do justly, to love mercy, and to walk humbly with God.*

Gerri spoke to the audience assembled virtually at the Innocence Project of the extraordinary human being whose passing we both mourned:

"Bobby Joe's case came at a time when there was not a public consciousness of wrongful convictions, and I still cannot understand or work out how somebody who went through what he went through, could come out on the other side of that with his humanity intact. It makes you understand that what makes a person's life meaningful and valuable is not always their education, their station in life, it's who you are as a human being."

When Gerri reviewed a draft of this book, she noted that Highway 82 ran through Reform Alabama to her hometown of Greenville Mississippi: "I had no idea of the straight line where Bobby Joe and I grew up. Symmetry in a way.

"That highway scared me one day when I was driving alone at dusk trying to make it from Greenville to Atlanta. White men in a pickup truck with a gunrack drove behind me for many, many miles. I was sure they were waiting for the moment to run me off the road at a place where no one would ever find me My lucky day when they turned off to go on their way not giving a thought to the terrified Black girl."

Before her retirement, as the first African American woman appointed to the state's highest court, Gerri authored decisions that brought attention to many who did not share her life experiences, but who welcomed her wisdom. In one, critiquing the so-called stop and frisk policy, she wrote that young Black men may flee from police, not because they are engaged in wrongdoing, but because of distrust resulting from *the recurring indignity of racial profiling.* It caught the attention of many judges, prosecutors, and police.

To those inspired "young people," the passionate lawyer and the wise judge, Bobby Joe's life and experience sparked understanding and commentary of social, criminal, and racial justice.

Gerri's observation of young Black men interacting with police also prompted me to recall a speech given by Supreme Court Justice William Brennan decades earlier, when he commented: *Nothing rankles more in the human heart than a brooding sense of injustice.*

That leaves those of us who are so interested , who care about it and are sorting out all the hate, violence and social confusion that seems to never go away, to ponder what we should do in the face of a *brooding sense of injustice.* What can be done?

In spite of my early apprehension about burning out, I remain a teacher. Michael Taylor, who directed Bobby Joe to his job as a Street Worker, is the president of Boston's Urban College, a fabulous institution that provides life changing education to the most underserved population in Greater Boston. He invited me to serve as an adjunct professor, teaching *Law and Justice.*

Boston College Law School has not tired of me after seventeen years and I continue, like an acting coach, teaching Trial

Practice. Boston Latin School has invited me back several times to speak about Bobby Joe in a building much modernized, but with the same spirit I felt on my first day of class three weeks before Bobby's arrest when I was a twenty-two-year-old "Junior Master." I have made regular appearances at my Alma Mater, B.C. High, and recently received a thumb's up and an "A Plus" from Michael Gardner who arranged the sessions. I told him: "I wish my mother was alive. It's the first "A" I ever got. She would be so proud!" In the summer of 2021, Jerry and Vanessa brought me back for my 28th appearance before the Judicial Youth Corp.

I tell students, mostly the "young people" that Bobby favored, that they can draw from his example. He called a few, like myself, his *brother,* but also treated everyone else as one. Teenagers in classrooms and on the streets need the reassurance that treating others with respect, as their equals *endowed by their creator with certain unalienable rights*, is not just the *right* thing to do, but often the easiest, and always the most beneficial.

I tell my law students that learning the mechanics of a civil and a criminal trial requires study and practice but discharging the highest ethical obligations of a lawyer requires character and values. I remind them that they should draw inspiration from our constitutional tenets, but always be aware of their flaws, and during their lifetimes in this noble profession, they should strive to improve the law, and the lives that the law serves; and that all begins in our courtrooms.

They are the sacred chambers: Impartial juries can be seated; admissible evidence can be presented; disputed evidence can be challenged; truthfulness, not totally guaranteed, can be secured under oath and with the threat of jail for perjurers. And don't think judges are potted plants: they are pretty good referees and safeguard due process of law.

More than a few students have heard me compare the power of advocacy to Archimedes' reputed dictum, *Give me a place to stand and with my lever I will move the world.* It is the leverage I was referencing when I told the spouse of a federal judge: *Judges have responsibility. Lawyers have all the power.* I also tell them that trying cases is a lot of fun.

It has been many decades since my morning at the South Boston District Court, when I responded to a judge's directive, as the first of many black robed curators of fairness and equal protection of law intimidated that young lawyer. I now call dozens of judges my very good friends, including those with the title Chief Justice, and from time to time, without hesitation, and always with respect, I remind them of Bobby Joe's prescient words:

I think I bring God to everyone in the court. I think they all know God should be looking over their work. I guess I remind them.

Yes, Bobby Joe, you do.

June 23, 2019, last meeting with JYC students in the Single Justice Session, Massachusetts Supreme Judicial Court..

www.ingramcontent.com/pod-product-compliance
Lightning Source LLC
Chambersburg PA
CBHW072138270326
41931CB00010B/1805